Stress Ma
Calm and
Overwhelmed

MW00941496

How to Getting More Done to Stop Anxiety, Improve Your Mood and Achieving Your Goals

accounting or official statements. If legal or professional advice is needed, a professional in the field must request it.

Table of Content

Introduction

Thank you for downloading this special guide titled *"Stress Management: Be Calm and Stop Feeling Overwhelmed."*

You can't seem to do anything about your stress level. Bills will not stop piling, daily tasks continue to increase, and responsibilities will be more demanding. But you can always be in charge. In fact, the simple understanding that you have control over your life is the basis of stress management.

Stress management has to do with responsibility: the responsibility of your thoughts, feelings, plans, environment and how to handle issues.

The ultimate goal of a balanced life is through work, relationships, relaxation and entertainment, in addition to resisting pressure and facing challenges.

You have the option to explode or prosper, let alone control your stress and weaken it or use it to gain greater power and happiness. It is left for you to seek value outside of yourself and constantly feel hopeless or lacking or seek to know its value from within. It is up to you to decide if you want to be happy in the future or choose happiness because, ultimately, you can make the decision using stress yourself.

Know that stress is natural and necessary because you can act when there is a threat to balance. The problem is that when stress causes negative emotions, negative emotions can overwhelm you and disconnect you from your upper brain and your reasoning, and they can behave in a way that is often annoying to others or to yourself. The deeper your pain, the stronger your negative emotions will be and the greater the negative reaction. Trying to stop the reaction is often almost impossible, like trying to stop the cold when it's cold outside.

What happens if you start seeing stress differently? If you knew that every time you feel stressed or distressed, that is, the stress associated with a negative emotion, do you really receive an alert signal that you are emptying and need refueling?

If you had to deal with a different anguish, react less or nothing, you have the opportunity to heal the part of you that has fractured. The less you feel broken, the more you generalize. The more you have, the less emotion and anxiety you will have. You have more balance within yourself and your life. You feel good and inevitably you are much happier. The happier and clearer you are, the more successful you will be.

The solution is to get what you need and get rid of the "not enough" syndrome. The more complete and balanced you are, the less stimulated you will be and the more likely you will find happiness.

Do you remember a time when you felt blessed? You should try to think of moments when you feel at ease, around the world, happy, calm. Maybe you have been on vacation. Or maybe you've been playing for five years. Or maybe that was the moment you fell in love. The happiness you have already felt. You know you have and as you've already felt, you can certainly feel it again.

The way to happiness is freedom. I am not referring to freedoms that are in no way being responsible to others or to yourself, but to freedom that comes from not being connected to your properties, people, feelings and suffering.

This kind of freedom means giving up on things, beliefs or ideas that you think will determine your worth and happiness.

This is the type of freedom you get once you feel good because you opt to try it, not because you're expecting something or somebody else to try it.

When you don't get absorbed by your expectations, crazy stories, or beliefs about what life is all about, you'll find freedom. you'll be proud of this freedom.

Happiness lies in your ability to specialize in feeling good and feeling fortunate about the way you think about yourself. This doesn't mean that your goal is to suppress emotions. Instead, the goal is to find out to interrupt free from negative emotions, to be less on top of things in order that you'll heal and feel comfortable. Once you feel comfortable, people and negative situations won't really bother you much.

In this special guide - ***Stress Management: Be Calm and Stop Feeling Overwhelmed***, I've explained everything you need to know to stay calm, cool and avoid bumps. This book teaches you specific tools to help you understand the cause of anxiety and how to release it and discover ways to create happiness.

Let's get started!

Why Stress Management is Crucial for Success

We can define stress as psychological or emotional stress caused by adverse or very demanding situations (for example, when one is under a lot of stress) that causes such a situation.

The fact is that stress is widespread. There is no way to avoid it, destroy it or desire it. Stress is a very real part of life. Its effect can be felt greatly and, therefore, must be treated.

If you are at work, stress is so common for clips and bills. Healthy stress levels can play a role in your business, taking you and your employees and colleagues to creative solutions and pushing you towards deadlines.

However, when stress becomes an overwhelming force, it can be debilitating. Stress can cause involuntary damage to your employees and your company. Statistics in Canada estimates the annual cost of work-related stress at more than $ 12 billion annually.

Stress management means our ability to control situations where conditions, people and events overwhelm us. This is the key to happiness. It is your ability to effectively manage the pressures you feel at work and at home. It's about knowing your limits.

Before addressing other important aspects of stress management, we will consider some of the reasons why stress management is so important for success in life.

Stress Management Can Help Prevent Stress

An old saying here comes to mind that "the problem that is in common is reduced by half." Because one of the main stressors of being stressful is that it starts as something very minor. Whatever the problem, it is often the "under the carpet" that hopes to resolve itself, which rarely happens. As such, it leaves it and becomes a much bigger problem.

When dealing with stress, you can stop stress immediately, before the stress begins to decrease. Which of the actions we take and how much we improve depends on the time, the nature of the stress and, of course, for each of us because we are all different.

Stress Management Helps to Examine the True Cause of Stress

This often does not seem easy. Often, the cause of stress is not really what one thinks. For example, the stress of traveling to work every morning is not our main stressor. A co-worker or maybe just a random thing can cause such, but we've been tricked into believing that this is often the most explanation for stress because it's the only solution.

With the rest of our devices, we may not even begin to resolve this stress and possibly dismiss it as a major problem.

Stress Management Will Help to Reveal Coping Strategies

Getting to the bottom of stress is part of stress management, but it is another equally important part of the process to achieve future stress management techniques. Often, it is helpful to speak with a stress management specialist and at first relieve existing stress. It is of little use if one becomes stressed again in the near future. Therefore, stress management provides a means to provide the necessary skills to get rid of future stress, with skills designed for each person. Therefore, this stress management can not only improve future well-being but also the future.

Stress Management Allows Us to Professionals Freely

Talking about anything with family and close friends, especially stress, can be difficult. We may be concerned that family members simply tell us that they love us and it doesn't matter, friends can be very partial, especially if it is a family member or another close friend that causes stress and we may not like to tell them to our colleagues for fear of appearing weak or unreliable.

Also, if there is employment in the current market, we may want to risk losing our job if it is transferred to the workplace if we talk about the stress we are going through. Talking with a professional stress management professional here has several benefits:

— All information is kept confidential so that we can be as open as we want to discuss everything.
— Above all, an experienced professional will also be completely neutral.

Therefore, don't be afraid to say something that bothers another family member or other professional. They simply sit and judge the situation based on their individual merits and offer the best possible advice for the whole situation.

The following are other important reasons for investing in stress management for you, your employees and co-workers, and the benefits of the company that can be derived from having healthy workers happy:

— This increases the staff's energy level and leads to team dynamics.

— This helps employees sleep better, increasing their productivity while working.

— This motivates employees to help them focus on tasks.

— This reduces staff stress, which leads to increased alertness.

— This reduces blood pressure and increases the quality of work of employees.

— This creates a positive outlook and increases your presence at work.

These are the reasons why, in my profession, stress management is a positive action that should be taken if you suffer from stress. As I said earlier, stress management can not only help with current stress, but it can also help address other important concerns, which may not even be met and can actually stop the techniques. To create the future. The stress of building

By investing in stress management, you will understand how your company can benefit from these rewards and many more. You and your employees will feel alive in control of your stress and power. You can also work to incorporate a stress management plan into your job responsibilities and create a positive outlook for it. Because when we reduce stress, everyone wins. You become happier and more productive, that's why your work becomes more successful and you can progress further on the path to success.

Understanding Stress and its Relation to Negative Emotions

Over the years, I have come to believe that most people on this planet live their lives in fear of death, whether or not they truly love, and forbid their ability to live a full and beautiful life.

The reason the majority sleep in fear of death is because they do not agree or believe that they're truly loved or appreciated, or don't know their worth.

When people are truly loved, once they acknowledge their intrinsic value, value and importance, they're likely to require care of themselves and their environment. They experience fewer health problems, feel less emotionally and emotionally altered, and ultimately less anxious, afraid and angry.

Think about it: If you really loved yourself and knew what you were worth, could you not do all you could to nourish your body, mind, soul and soul? If you feed yourself so much that you feel valued and overlooked, you won't be happy, and if someone else doesn't care or even insults you, they will offend you.

Of course you want!

You have the power to be really happy, which ability resides in your body.

You have an outsized body made from billions of cells, some strong and a few weak. regardless of what their strength is, these cells help one another, protect one another from harm and align with one another to offer them an opportunity to measure legendary on this earth.

When these cells are not properly nourished, cared for or supported, they cannot fully support him for life and shine, for happiness and success.

The beauty of your body is that it always lets you know when you need it, when you want to help or when it changes. Symptoms come in the form of feelings such as hunger or fatigue, cough, discomfort, or negative emotions or thoughts. These symptoms tell you when you are in stress or when you are safe, out of balance or out of balance, restless or in a state of peace and love. The food you eat, the people you spend time with, the movements you make, the thoughts you hold, or the words you say have a positive or negative impact on each of your cells. In turn, these cells tell you whether your actions will help you progress or dive.

If you pay attention, you love yourself, you really want to be happy, you listen to your body's signals and defend the behaviors and actions that make you dive, and only help those who help you progress. They defend you.

You have a choice. You have the choice every day and every moment of your life whether you want to nourish or hurt your body and body. The less hurt you are, the less the world can hurt you.

You can see your life by appreciating experiences that help you discover your true self, living your life to the best of your being or expressing regret over not having enough. See yourself. That you feel your life as a victim of your own circumstances.

You have the choice of believing within the greatness of your being that it can't be undermined by another, otherwise you can believe that your existence is useless which you'll be great as long as you're known or valued by the opposite.

If you're proud of your choice, all you've got to try to is start listening to your body's signals.

Understanding Stress

Your body speaks to you in stress. Stress is that the reason we produce, innovate, run marathons and advertise. this is often how we get out of bed within the morning and have an incentive to place food on the table.

When something within us wants to vary, it drives us to try it. The tendency to change is due to stress. Do you feel tired? Pressure. Are you hungry? Pressure. Low blood pressure? Stress again.

Stress is not necessarily bad. You need it to help you live, adapt and survive. It motivates us to climb mountains or innovate and find new ways to be easier or reach faster.

Stress is defined as any problem with balance (also known as homeostasis). The challenges can range from simple climate change to global news, fatal deadlines, pollution, colds, changes in blood pressure, hunger, fatigue, inflammation, lack of sleep, eating processed foods or emotional stress.

Stress can manifest itself as a challenge that endangers real life or hidden stressors, such as worrying action, feeling deficient or a defective immune system that cannot respond to strong antibodies.

For the brain, anything that tackles the body's homeostasis is eligible for stress, and it doesn't matter if it's physical, mental, emotional, real or imaginary. As long as the brain understands that its balance is being challenged, stress is considered, and in doing so, a physiological response to stress is always mounted to solve the problem, so that it can adapt and stay alive.

The Stress Response

There are several quality reasons for a stress response or a physiological response to stress. It lifts one from bed in the morning, tells the immune system to fight off infections, the blood vessels to maintain blood pressure, and your body to move during discomfort and the sensory system to alert for hunger, cold or tiredness. Without a response to stress, you will actually be dead because it will heal wounds, survive injuries, meet nutritional needs and escape when a lion chases you.

Walter Kanon, a Harvard physiologist, preferred the term " fight or flight" in the 1930s to describe our innate defense response to threat or danger. He believed that this defense would ultimately guarantee survival. When we are in danger or in danger, we move into the bloodstream due to the release of stress hormones such as adrenaline and cortisol, which causes our senses to become too alert and excited. Our students tense to dilute and our muscles to prepare for battle or flight.

The liver releases sugar stored in the bloodstream to nourish your body, while the lungs work faster, increasing your breathing speed and making your breathing more superficial than oxygen consumption. The heart pumps harder and faster, blood pressure increases and the immune system is stimulated to mount an inflammatory response to protect it from scars or possible infections.

It is a great physiological response to be chased after by a tiger, and in the short term it will often cause physical, emotional or psychological distress of one kind or another to serve you. For example, if your blood sugar level drops, the stress response will trigger a series of physiological changes that will make you feel hungry, irritable or tired. This discomfort or negative feeling forces him to eat something to eliminate hunger or discomfort so he can regain his balance or comfort. Eating food can relieve stress so that it no longer has to be a stress response. The stress response itself turns off and allows your system to resume its stable state.

This is good news when dealing with stress and responding to stress. The bad news is that your brain can't tell the difference between stress and the other.

He cannot differentiate between running for his life and delaying his work because they both pose a threat to his livelihood somewhere in his brain. For this reason, too much stress is often activated, and in most cases, because of constant worry, it never disappears because the stress never goes away.

Perception Is Key

At this time, you may think that because you are always stressed, you are condemned, meaning that your response to stress is always active, so you are either angry or ill. Don't despair. She has the ability to solve the problem by learning how to change her perceptions of her life and her life.

The key to keeping a stress response under control is understanding. If your brain realizes that a particular situation is manageable, it triggers a stress response long enough to trigger the necessary actions, such as an athlete motivated to compete and win a race. In fact, this is what you want with a positive outlook. Positive understanding is directly related to homeland security or confidence in the success or ability to manage a particular effort or challenge. In contrast, negative perceptions are associated with low self-esteem and belief in the probability of a positive outcome.

For example, you can apologize for choosing a school for your child. You abuse this problem day and night until you feel that your life is out of control. Your anxiety stimulates the stress response, it increases your heart rate and blood pressure, the inflammation flows through your body, your memory increases your sense of blur and your cravings for comfort food or alcohol. You feel tired, in pain and overwhelmed with the desires of your life. You just don't think you can do more. Then, the child, spouse, boss, or person who fills the vacuum cleaner acts cruelly or excessively and your temper is used by you and others. The shame you experience makes you feel worse, the stress response intensifies and the cycle goes on.

Now if you can change your mindset to believe that whatever choice you make is good, the scenario will be very different.

For example, you are very confident about your ability to make decisions and you also believe that there is no wrong choice as each option provides opportunities for growth and learning. You know that no matter what school you send your child to, it will be great or you will find ways to make it work. She has an attitude similar to most of her life's desires, because she knows who to provide and help when needed. In this case, do you think you will explode when it is said that a boy, a wife, a boss, or someone who is filling in the papers is being ruthless? Probably not. Why? ... perception.

When you consider stress to be controllable, you control the response to stress and its reactions. Understanding is really the key to resilience. The more you believe in your own ability and resources to deal with profanity, the more likely you find stress manageable, which will lead to less worries, more confidence, a greater sense of worth, a positive expectation, a controlled stress response. And you are stronger

If you want to benefit from a positive understanding that resources are available to access any uncertainty, you will intervene with more confidence and know that you can handle whatever is in your way. You can maintain a sense of calm, even if someone acts cruelly or disrespectfully. Your stress level is controlled. Sustainable physical health and mental and emotional clarity, intact.

Consciousness Leads to A Better Understanding

If it were easy to keep positive control of stress control under control, I would not want to write this book or have a job. The important thing is that you must be aware of your stress and take care of it before controlling it. For example, you may not realize that the lack of sleep you experience as a result of striving to succeed in the workplace can cause inflammation in your body and cause more stress. You may also be aware that you keep memories that no longer serve you. These memories still define you and your understanding and lead you to success at the expense of the body. In the end you may not realize that you are not good enough and that you have had constant stress throughout your life.

Awareness of Emotions and Memories

Emotions and emotional memory are directly correlated with physiological, positive and negative responses. Every time you experience certain emotions, your brain looks for its emotional memory bank to boost physiological and physical assumptions, beliefs, behaviors and reactions that help you cope with the past. When you face challenges that make you feel good, your brain looks for details of your memory bank to see how those challenges have been made before, what resources have been used and what the results are. It has been and the information corresponds to your emotional memory bank. The result is a response and behavior to the challenge created by current unconscious belief and assumption.

Throughout life, as one memory is reinforced over another, a belief system is formed about how you see yourself, others and the world around you, if you have enough and if you have enough and if You are negative or negative. From this point of view. It is not enough or not enough. Most people have different opinions depending on the circumstances. For example, the same person may believe that there will always be enough money because he is rich, but there is never enough love because there is no love at home. Therefore, some of his ideas support positive expectations that his future needs will be met. Other beliefs, based on more annoying experiences, take a more negative stance and maintain negative expectations that you may never have or have enough, and you cannot rely on the world or people to help you.

This leads to circumstances that come up nowadays where positive or negative physiological responses re produced, and subsequent beliefs and behaviors supported memory.

For example, if in the past your family always had enough money and all your needs were always met, you probably believe today that you will always get enough of what you need. Conversely, if he grew up raising food on his desk and clothes, but his parents were constantly worried about money, he would likely share some of that concern. Now as an adult, even if you have a steady income, you may still be asking yourself, "What if I don't get it? What if I don't have enough money?" You worry about it every day and stay in a job you don't like even if you dream of doing something else, and you basically feel overwhelmed. (Do you see how this can be a source of dissatisfaction, frustration, and an easy explosion?)

Another example could be that your boss, colleague or friend disrespects you or does not follow your advice.

If he was often criticized in the past, this kind of situation could make him much angrier than someone who was rarely criticized. Whenever they criticize you, this memory is activated. When you are activated, you do what you have always done to fight: you scream, you eat, you pick, and so on. Although this behavior helps you deal with it in the short term, it does not solve anything and in the end it usually feels worse.

Belief Consciousness

Always remember that this is not your memory and what has happened to you in the past is not worth it. The problem is, when you were a kid, you still didn't have much brain. In other words, when bad things happen to you, your brain interprets the situation based on limited knowledge and skills. The belief from this point of view was often distorted and incorrect. It is an irrational and false belief that drives you to respond to stress and negative behaviors.

If he had consciously focused on changing his beliefs so that a new person would eventually act in a more positive, rational, and realistic way, he would have been better able to manage his reaction and stress.

There are many techniques in the psychological and psychological worlds, including cognitive reconstruction strategies and a variety of meditation techniques, which I will discuss in this book.

The argument is that you can simply change your views in a negative or positive way. It is possible to separate negative emotions and perceptions from unpleasant memories and reprogram the brain with positive emotions and standards of confidence.

You can learn to understand situations differently to control them. Most importantly, you can learn to see yourself differently, love and support them by knowing that you are truly valuable. When you do, it can shake you very little.

Being in Control

When my patients decide to be self-sufficient, I found that they become healthier, more resilient, and more calm to maladaptation. Patients who are victims of living conditions, on the other hand, are less likely to face serious challenges and are more likely to be exposed to negative emotional, psychological and physical complaints.

Always remember that with the choices you make and the perceptions you can make, especially with regard to stress in life and how it is generally viewed in the world, you can make your life positive or negative. Impress. When you maintain a positive mentality or understanding, keep the stress response under control and work from the place where you feel happy and happy in the face of tiredness and anger. You feel in control.

Your ability to maintain a positive mentality and understanding depends on three factors:

— Your past experiences, memories, and beliefs, especially how you feel about yourself and your resources. As I briefly explained above, they affect your understanding, especially when you are in a negative mood.

— Your mood, positive or negative. I hope you have noticed the difference in your mood and emotional state as a result of your self-awareness.

— Your support infrastructure, that encourages you to have an open mind and agile body and know you've got what you need to succeed and flourish. This network encompasses how long you sleep, how well you care about yourself (e.g., fitness, diet, meditation), how good the social support group is, how often you play and joke, how well you are linked to spiritual work and values, and how you spend time in nature.

As you read on, I will provide you with tools and techniques that will help you improve your beliefs, maintain a positive spirit, and build your infrastructure. You will learn to calm your mind and calm your body to reject stress, while you learn to be sympathetic and not to judge that you feel activated. You will learn to be aware of your body's emotions, thoughts, and physiological reactions, rather than react to them, guide them, and ultimately unbind yourself. Eventually you will learn how to access feelings of happiness, love, and compassion. To find your strength and it doesn't matter because you find your happiness.

Become Aware of Your Stressors

Stress is part of regular and even healthy life. While it may be useful in many situations, it is harmful in others. Understanding the subtleties of stress and a proper understanding of its causes and effects can help you use this book.

This chapter provides an overview of different types of stress and the main effects of stress on the body, mind, and overall health. You can also discover the most effective ways of using the book and apply what you are doing and get the most of it.

The cause of tension is evident as we face an immediate deadline, a difficult social situation or an urgent obstacle. But most of the time, we experience stress from multiple sources and less experience about where the stress comes from and how it affects us.

As someone who reads a book on stress management, you probably know that stress can make a difference in your life. So why have I included a full chapter on how to become aware of stress? Because we need to understand where our stress comes from, and how it affects us, we know what to do to control it. And our understanding of the source of stress is sometimes less clear than it seems. In fact, understanding the amount of stress can be surprisingly difficult.

When our lives are relatively stress-free, a stressful event is highlighted. In a low stress lifestyle, a new stressor shows a conflict with what we are used to, so we know the stress that comes with it is very easy and we know where the stress comes from. However, when faced with a growing number of stressors (from acute to episodic stress), we tend to eliminate much more.

It is more difficult to identify some of the causes of stress in our lives. First, with several sources of stress, we can feel "disordered". We can name some of our sources of stress, perhaps the most pressing and most obvious ones, but we can overlook some of the other nuances of life. That gives us stress.

This chapter will describe in detail the signs and symptoms of stress. It examines shared resources, such as jobs, relationships, and terrible programs. This chapter lets you get to know the sources of stress and its effects better, and ask questions that can help you evaluate your stress level so you can have a clear idea of how to combat it.

Stress can come from many sources and can affect people in many ways. Ending a relationship can be a liberating experience for one person and an overwhelming experience for the other. Even the experience of sitting at a desk and working while the sound of birds and lawnmowers coming through an open window can be relaxing for one person and frustrating for the other. Given this diversity, we cannot say with certainty that experiences are inherently stressful for all, and to what extent.

Reportedly, studies have shown that specific experiences are felt by many to be particularly stressful and that special situations are often experienced as stressful. Below are some of the main sources of stress that people usually experience.

This is not a comprehensive list, but when you see stress in your life, there are some famous culprits here.

Work

Many people cite work as one of the biggest stressors and there are many reasons for this. Since most of us spend most of our time in the workplace, jobs are often closely linked to our personal identity, finances, and lifestyle. This makes our work greatly influenced by our general well-being. People with specific occupations are at greater risk of stress and also at increased risk of fatigue, anxiety, and depression. These are some of the most serious stressors at work.

— Low Recognition: When workers are uncertain about the scope of their responsibilities, they make it difficult to fulfill these obligations. This is obvious, but there are many working conditions with unclear requirements, where workers know that only when the problem arises is something gone. When people aren't sure what their jobs mean, they may be asked to do things that are not their responsibility, and may not be sure if they can afford to do so. They can work hard all day and never know if they have worked hard enough. They may be insecure or angry and don't know what to do about it. Especially when authorities do not have clear communication, this can indicate stressful dynamics.

In difficult economic times, when companies are shrinking and workers remaining responsible for jobs previously held by others, this can become an even bigger problem. Individuals may be forced to do other jobs previously hired, or may feel that their jobs will be jeopardized if they do not perform additional duties. This can put extra pressure on a currently stressful job situation.

If you are in a job where the requirements are unclear, you may not even realize that this is an important source of stress: you could sincerely be aware that you're feeling burdened at work and now not positive the way to satisfy all of the demands.

If unspecified job descriptions are part of the problem, be sure to talk to the person in charge and see if you can get written explanations. If you are a self-employed individual, make certain to talk with every different and clarify your expectations together with your client, telling them what they can anticipate from you.

— Low Recognition: In other work situations, the demands are clear but impossible to fulfill. Workers are expected to do more than time permits or do things that they do not need. This kind of situation is frustrating because workers feel overwhelmed and eventually give up. Situations like these can pose a threat to self-esteem, a sense of safety at work, and waiting for any sense of accomplishment.

Again, this is a situation where self-awareness becomes very important. People in stressful jobs may feel overwhelmed if they feel that the demands are unattainable and are doing something about it. They may feel that the task is tedious and difficult, but understanding that being realistic is not able to complete it can be a relief.

It is useful if you may take a look at your scenario objectively and see that the expectancies you are being imposed aren't realistic. Perhaps the worst issue we can do is to stand up to unrealistic desires and decide ourselves as opposed to recognizing while something is certainly not viable.

If you are in a working environment where you think the demands are unrealistic, it is important to talk to your boss about it and see if you can objectively show that the job may not be rational. If you are a freelance worker, you may have to talk to yourself and set your expectations. Communicating with customers and setting boundaries is also important. Since trying to meet impossible demands can be very daunting and can cause tiredness and depression, this is a situation that should be possible in every way.

— **Low Recognition**: Working conditions that reduce compensation, are considered serviceable, or otherwise do not reward the effort required can be daunting and stressful. When things happen in the workplace that cause people to feel disrespected for what they are doing, it can damage their self-esteem, motivation and motivation, and make work feel challenging and eroding. Slow. It does not necessarily mean self-satisfaction, but rather a sense of value. Feeling unfair about being ignored by advertising; Feeling displeased by a manager, colleague or customer. And it is the feeling of exploiting stressful emotions that can help with chronic stress and job dissatisfaction.

If you feel a lack of knowledge in your work, there may be ways to create recognition in your life without having to change jobs to get it. If you are not working with your company manager, boss or HR manager, you can create a support network for friends and colleagues and congratulate each other on your achievements. Consider having a regular lunch session where everyone shares what they are proud of (and in turn gets behind) or enjoys other challenges with their own challenges. This may seem unnecessary, but therapists and educators often have support groups like this because they can be very helpful. You can also simply have a friend or two support them so you can exchange celebratory phone conversations. Another option is to have some fun outside the workplace to provide the positive feedback we all need, even if it is not about your accomplishments. It is worth noting that lack of appreciation can be stressful in any job and can be a step towards controlling that stress.

Another option that can be quite effective in relieving stress in such situations is to find a deeper meaning in your work. If you can identify ways in which your interests are beneficial to others, for example, work becomes more important than just tasks performed and tasks become more important, even if the tasks themselves are not inherently pleasant.

High Penalty for Errors

In areas such as medicine or transportation, there is necessarily a narrow line of error: If it goes wrong, people can die. These are not the only areas where there are negative consequences associated with errors. Some companies dismiss people because of small mistakes, some managers make mistakes, and at other times the consequences are part of the work that cannot be changed. Freelancers and business owners can lose the customer when they make small mistakes, and those dissatisfied customers can express their dissatisfaction.

Whether this is a punishment for a company decision or just part of the job, the working conditions that cause a few errors can be frustrating. They can keep us in a state of constant alertness and create a sense of doubt and insecurity. After some time, the pressure may get its effects.

In addition to taking care of ourselves, we can perform best and manage yourself in the most effective way possible to manage situations such as the one above Explained, did. We can be more stressed than such.

— **Lack of Challenge**: Work seems to relieve intolerable stress, but some non-challenging jobs may be more stressful than those with higher levels of challenge. This is because we are naturally inclined to grow and may feel we can do something that harnesses our unique strengths. People tend to feel less stressed when doing things that show a good level of challenge, not as stressful as they are, but not too low to be painful and dull. Those who work in jobs that are not repetitive and cure may find themselves afraid of going to work. It's not as stressful as some of the others discussed here, but it can certainly have its side effects.

If you are in a job that does not take advantage of or challenge you, it can be a simple correction. Spending time to the entertainment that challenges you when you're not working can provide the stimulation you need to feel more balanced throughout your life. In this case, more of the challenge means less stress.

Relationships

Relationships can carry us the great and the worst moments. Although it is often useful to our fitness and wellbeing, our relationships can also create barriers which can be often mentioned as key factors in lifestyle's strain.

While discussing the interaction between relationships and stress, there are several important points that can be remembered during a relationship as stressful. The following are types of relationships that can be stressful.

— Toxic relationships: Having relationships that are not respected is very stressful. When exposed to repeated criticism, unsubstantiated gossip, unrealistic demands, humiliation, ridicule and other negative experiences, when we don't feel safe, we may not understand the numbers that come from us. Similarly, in relationships where we feel we are not the best, it is bad not only for us but also for other people in our lives. We can get used to the scenario, we won't be capable of discover the damage we're doing, and we are able to forget about to do something to trade the state of affairs we are in.

The relationships that generally make us feel bad about ourselves can be a source of constant stress because they can lead to negative rumors, low self-esteem, conflicts for continuous resolution and other threats to happiness and self-esteem. Be us

— **Caregivers**: Those who are responsible for the continued well-being of their loved ones are particularly stressed, varying in severity depending on the needs of the caregivers. Regardless of whether caregivers can love their family members, responsibilities can be discharged and feelings related to them can exacerbate work-related stress.

When children are young, they need almost constant attention and participation. Studies show that marital satisfaction decreases in those early years as parents strive to meet these demands. While young children are ideally in close contact with their parents or guardians, nutrition, change, search, tobacco and other demands that are part of the care of young children can produce the necessary effects and stress.

People who care for relatives of the sick, disabled or elderly often have high levels of stress. In fact, this type of stress can cost more. First, it is extremely difficult to deal with the fact that a loved one needs continuous support. Caregivers feel for their loved ones and prefer to see them as healthy and capable for their own good.

Caring can also be difficult for these loved ones, and caregivers often have this feeling, they may feel guilty for feeling stressed. The workload can be even more difficult than caring for young children because it can be unexpected, emotionally exhausting and physically demanding more treatment for an adult who needs their primary care, medical procedures and other challenges, Se.

If they are taken care of, they may feel tired and drowned, caregivers may be more stressed. However, even the most loving caregivers are human, and sometimes demands to meet someone else's needs can affect our ability to meet our personal needs.

Getting support, both emotional and practical, and taking the time to take care of your stress management is crucial at this stage. Ideally, the responsibility for care should be shared among several people so that nobody burns. The participation of siblings in the care of elderly parents or the sharing of responsibilities between spouses and perhaps the use of external resources in the care of children with special needs can ensure that each caregiver has the opportunity to adequately address their needs. However, there are not always other people willing or able to help. Fortunately, there are support groups for parents and caregivers in the community, and access to these resources can change a lot. If you feel uncomfortable as a supervisor, I encourage you to do this now by researching resources (trusting others and trusting support groups in your community).

Hectic Schedules

It looks overwhelmed for many new normal people. We, as a society, have been more expectant of ourselves in recent years than in the files of previous generations. Many people work more than ever and often work on more than one job. We will not close during bids. A new survey shows that only 45% of respondents plan to use vacations during the summer, the lowest percentage in the survey's 11-year history, of which only 35% opted for longer trips. Expected to spend his weekends alone.

We fill our free time with extra responsibilities, and then we realize why we're tired (or maybe we wonder or maybe give up).

Being aware of the enormous speed of our lives may be the first step in creating a more appropriate lifestyle, but sometimes we need to take a serious look at our plans to know that we've been through a lot and know what activities we have. We do it to eliminate it. One way to have an honest view and start optimizing your plan is to create a complete plan for yourself, if you haven't done so already.

Instead of simply stating your core commitments, look for a calendar application that you can use on your computer (I like iCal and Google Calendar), and list the things that make up your agenda do. How long does blocking and labeling take you to get ready for the morning, how much time you spend driving and even your rest, and seeing where your time is spent.

To get a more accurate picture of your current time location, you can check out the calendar throughout the day and see if you really do what you want to plan every day. Drawing a meticulous plan like this can allow you to really see where your time is going and see more clearly where you can waste your time or identify what activities are truly meeting your goals and satisfaction. It's not your life.

Health

Stress and health are closely linked. As I mentioned earlier in this chapter, stress can affect our health, and health problems can cause significant stress. In fact, coping with health problems represents one of the biggest stressors people face. Hoping for more lives and more medical advances, we tend to experience chronic diseases (such as heart disease and cancer) of viral infections and diseases that have claimed lives more than a century ago (and interestingly). Almost all of these chronic diseases have either direct or chronic diseases (indirect links to stress, including other risk factors). The stress of living with chronic conditions and serious health threats can affect not only those who are experiencing stress, but also their friends and family. And conditions that are not more severe can also have its consequences.

The knowledge we need to take care of our health can affect our minds when over-stressed and pressured to make better decisions. The reality of dealing with a serious health condition is more stressful. The best we can do is use our time to stay healthy, get support whenever possible, and practice stress management techniques to support our overall health and well-being. Taking this book (and reading it) is the first important step you've taken. Following Key 3 recommendations for body care, and Key 8 recommendations for maintaining resilience promotion habits may be the best option to improve overall health and well-being.

Life Adjustments

As I mentioned earlier, one of the most striking characteristics of stress is that it is the result of any situation that needs to be answered. This means that events in our lives, both positive and negative, can cause stress, simply because of a response. Different life events cost more or less, but any event can cause stress. One of the most popular ways to measure stress in a person's life is to use the Holmes & Ra's Stress Scale (named by the psychologists who created it), which is the name of 43 stressful life events and its weight. Each is due to the level of stress and the likelihood of related illnesses. This scale is obtained by counting the "value" of each of the events that occurred last year. While this scale may not be an appropriate measure of stress (for example, divorce or death in the family may have more impact than another, depending on the relationships involved), this is a general and reliable measure. A clear basic picture. It also shows that any event in our lives can affect our overall stress levels.

The list includes clearly stressful events such as "spouse death", "divorce" and "imprisonment". Moderate stressors such as "change in reasoning" and "change in a different line of work" and relatively benign events such as "change in eating habits" and "holidays."

While the scale helps you get a clearer picture of the stress you experienced last year, simply seeing your life and assessing the events that caused the most stress will help you get more of your origin. be in contact. Stress can be effective because depending on personal factors and other problems in your life, you can have an accurate understanding of the impact of each event on you.

A look at the stressful events of the past year will also help you find a spirit that allows you to become more aware of and deal with your stressors. What kind of stressful events did you face last year and what do you think they cost?

Attitudes and Perspectives

We may not always understand it, but how we perceive and process our lives can in itself be a source of stress. When we look more at the negative aspects than the positive aspects of a situation, we can experience it as more threatening and therefore more stressful. When we stop at the negative things in our lives, we exacerbate the stress we feel. As we approach different situations in our lives as perfection races, feeling the need to overcome those around us and hit anything that is not ideally impossible, we can put unnecessary stress on ourselves and those around us.

If we do not understand that our thinking patterns can have an impact on our stress levels, we will be caught up in the dynamics that follow us wherever we go and experience stress in our lives.

Here are three main thought patterns:

— **Rumination**: This means stopping in the negative, especially when there is nothing you can do about it. It is natural to want to solve problems as they arise, but gossiping is a negative and unproductive way of thinking about the things in our lives that are currently causing stress. Ruminants can consume hours of what could be a more pleasant day.

— **Negative thinking**: Focus on a negative situation, expect the wrong things to happen, explain the positive things that happen in life: all of these are negative thinking patterns. If you focus on the pessimistic side of things, you can save a lot of stress if you stop. Paying attention to this pattern is the first step.

— **Cognitive distortions**: There are several types of cognitive distortions. The link between them is that they overlook a vital piece of reality and cause stress. These mental patterns distorted by the psyche are automatically designed to protect people from stressful realities. Unfortunately, they tend to create long-term stress over the current time. Keep in mind that if you start to ignore specific facts, convince yourself that you are "right" in situations without objective evidence, or distort what is objectively happening around you. In the face of things, the way they really exist is, in the end, less stressful.

Reverse Your Stress Response

When you experience stress, a fight or flight reaction begins. As stress increases, this long-term response activates and affects performance in a way that exacerbates stress levels and endangers our health.

This chapter describes the stress response and provides simple and effective strategies to stimulate the body's relaxation response, which returns the body to its propulsion function. At the end of this season, you will have the tools to relax in minutes.

Perhaps one of the most important ways to minimize the negative effects of chronic stress is to develop effective ways to reverse the stress response as soon as we discover that it is stimulated.

Because chronic stress occurs when the body remains in a state of constant stress, if we can learn to return the body to rest (stabilization or homeostasis) between challenging events, we can create more time for the body. To make it feels stressful and ineffective. It is better to practice our techniques to relax our body so that we can relax with a little effort and this can be automatic.

By learning the techniques of relaxation and reduction of chronic stress we experience, we can feel more comfortable in the present moment and also allow ourselves to avoid the negative effects of chronic stress that we experience otherwise. By regularly practicing relaxation techniques, we can minimize body stress without changing anything else. Together with other effective stress management techniques, relaxation techniques become more powerful.

With this in thoughts, let's take observe a number of the simplest and handiest relaxation strategies. Activities that physically relax the body can work well to manage stress, as they not only allow you to relax your body's stress response, but can also help you separate your physical reactions from stress. Emotional stress also helps, so over time, you may be less physically receptive. Coping with stress Each of the following relaxation techniques can work quickly alone and can bring more benefits if used repeatedly or with other stress relief techniques. As you read, think about situations in which you generally feel stressed and remember the notes on what techniques may be the best time for that moment.

Breathing Exercises

Relaxation breathing is one of my favorite techniques that I recommend and is something I use in my life. Breathing exercises are simple because they can be learned in minutes and practiced by almost anyone, including children and people with physical problems. These exercises are versatile and convenient because they can be practiced at almost any time (even during a stressful event) and can be modified to suit individual tastes. With exercising, relaxation respiration can be automated, so that relaxation turns into a country of immersion in preference to something that is performed with the help of someone or something else. Easy, comfortable and easy, respiration sports work.

What distinguishes the rest of the breath from the kind of breathing we do every day is subtle however significant. When everything runs smoothly and the body relaxes, we naturally breathe through the diaphragm, the abdomen contracts and contracts with each breath as the shoulders relax and relax. We breathe deeply, fill our lungs and breathe easily.

When we face stress and the stress response is triggered, we tend to breathe less. We become less involved in breathing, where our shoulders stand firm and rise and fall with our breathing, while our abdominal muscles can contract. We breathe faster because we don't get as much air as we need. These are in line with the changes that prepare us to fight or run fast, but they are not healthy for us. Unfortunately, some people breathe in this way all the time upon waking up.

The act of consciously releasing stress in the body and forcing our breath to mimic the slower breathing in which our body rests can help reverse the response to the stress of the body and, therefore, to our physical well-being. It can also help us relax emotionally because the body no longer responds to stress.

How breathing exercises can work for you

Breathing is a critical a part of yoga, so in case you are interested in getting to know this form of respiration directly from your teacher, taking one or yoga classes may be a good idea. The instructor can talk to you through the procedure and can help you recognize if adjustments had been made in your technique.

However, for most people, studying respiration patterns is sufficient stress alleviation and a clean and effective manner to examine the procedure. The following instructions offer a quick and easy manner to respire to a quieter kingdom:

— Find a quiet place to rest and relax.

— Focus in your respiratory. Relax your shoulders and permit them surround you. Quickly recognize that there's anxiety in the relaxation of your frame and permit it relaxation.

— Pay attention for your breathing. Superficial? Do your shoulders upward thrust and fall with each breath? If so, relaxation even greater until your breathing is slow, consistent and deep, and your stomach expands with each breath and contracts, even if you have to loosen up to allow it to be carried out comfortably. This is known as diaphragmatic respiration (as it comes out of your diaphragm), and this is the way we naturally nod off or while we relax.

— To further adjust your breathing, you may want to count on each breath, slowly resting at inhalations and slowly reaching eight with each exhalation, to maintain speed.

— When you feel you are breathing alone, you can stop counting and stop concentrating on changing your breathing. Instead of changing your breathing patterns at this point, just take care of yourself as you leave the body. You should feel relaxed for a few minutes. You should also have a clear memory of this type of breathing easier to breathe in order to move it in a relaxed future.

Visualization

Research shows that visualization affects both the body and the mind. When we are clearly involved in an activity, the brain cannot distinguish between what we imagine and what we really experience. The mind believes that it experiences what we are visualizing.

Our pulse may decrease or accelerate depending on what we believe we are experiencing and other reactions, including those that help calm us down.

Although it is a bit surprising that the mind is fully visualized and "believes" that these experiences are correct, the interesting thing is that the muscles involved in visualization are really involved. This is excellent for athletes and for people who speak in public and other challenges that require training and confidence to master, but can also be useful for relaxation purposes.

The visualization of stress management can work in several ways. First, mere imagination in situations that are less stressful than the one you are currently experiencing can get your attention and can lead you to replace thoughts that respond to your stress with thoughts. Begin to be able to naturally capture your relaxation response or at least stop stress if you are worried about things that have bothered you in the past or if you are worried about things to deal with in the future. It can be useful

Secondly, self-visualization gives you more relaxation, not only in the absence of stressful thoughts, but also in the presence of more relaxing and joyful thoughts. If you close your eyes and imagine yourself in a soft cloud, float over the noise of your life (instead of stressful in the workplace) or imagine being in a place where you always feel comfortable (Just like your favorite home chair), can encourage your body to feel the sensation that it usually feels in that environment. Visualizing the positive things that happen in your life can help you have more confidence to face the challenges and can help you break negative thinking habits.

Another benefit of visualization is that you can imagine your body more easily. If your heart is racing, you can display images that show a slow speed, such as a slow canoe ride. You can also directly imagine that your pulse is slowing. If you feel tension in your shoulders, you can visualize the tension that comes out of your body by drawing an image of the tension that leaves the body through the pores or by transferring the sensation of relaxation from head to toe, as if you were poured the cup of water and you washed your body. You have the idea.

Visualization can work very quickly to help reduce stress. This technique usually requires some privacy or quiet time to focus, but practicing can shorten the time it takes to work out and reinforce the response you feel. (For example, by practicing you can create a "happy place" for yourself, a mental image that you think will calm you down and help you relax. Over time, you can get used to Just think about your happy place.) What kind of imagery she can experiment with; later in this chapter, I will give examples to give you an idea. You can also download your recordings from the book's Web site, which can relieve stress by viewing

Progressive Muscle Relaxation (PMR)

Progressive Muscle Relaxation (PMR) is a method that focuses primarily on the muscles themselves. While it takes a long time to master it, even short PMR sessions can provide more relaxation. The idea of PMR is to create stress and relaxation of all major muscle groups systematically and to discharge residual stress muscles in the process. With exercise, you can more easily relax your body in this way, often in minutes instead of minutes, a technique known as deep muscle relaxation (DMR). Learning PMR and DMR is relatively easy, but requires practice. Learning is more effective than a professional, though you can also learn from recordings and videos. Here is a simple version of PMR that you can now try:

— Book for a few minutes, find a private place away from distraction, and sit or lie down in a quiet position.

— Tighten your scalp muscles. Keep these muscles tired for at least 30 seconds, raise your ears (if possible) and press as much as possible. Then relax. Allow stress to drain from the muscles in your head, and simply "be".

— Repeat with your facial muscles. Hold the cheek muscles, jaw and the rest of the face as tightly as possible and hold it for about a minute. Then relax and let all the tension get out of your muscles.

— Repeat with your neck. Then move to the shoulders, arms, arms and fists, back, abdomen, buttocks, thighs, calves and legs.

— Over time, you can tighten any area more quickly and the relaxation process will be felt automatically.

Self-Hypnosis

When the idea of hypnosis sleep comes up, many people still think about the hypnosis that emerges on the scene: artists who volunteer to be hypnotized and volunteered, causing them to hear the word marshmallow or perform abnormal fears of power to behave like a chicken. Many of the techniques used in hypnosis, especially self-hypnosis, are much less shameful and are very helpful in helping participants change the behaviors they want to change. Hypnosis itself acts like a visualization, except that it is a deeper state of relaxation and a deeper commitment to the mind.

We can hypnotize ourselves for many purposes such as quitting smoking and relieving anxiety and phobia. But hypnosis itself is a particularly powerful tool for managing stress. You can take advantage of your subconscious mind and make suggestions that allow you to relax, let everything go out of your way, and maintain habits that relieve stress. To get the maximum effect, it usually takes a few sessions, but it can get you started quickly. A few minutes of relaxation can work well.

There are several different ways to use hypnosis and self-hypnosis to relieve stress. You can find many of your Hypnosis resources online, and you can create your own script and recordings.

Short Meditation

Meditation is a very powerful tool for stress management. This is best done for at least 15 or 20 minutes per workout because the mind is needed to calm down and this is a mind-numbing exercise and still offers many of the most remarkable benefits of meditation.

Shorter meditations (meditation sessions lasting 3-5 minutes) can also be helpful in reducing stress, as they can minimize your response to stress and help you relax your mind quickly. Just a few minutes of focusing inside can help you stop focusing on stressful situations around you.

Autogenic Training

Autogenic training can be very helpful to quickly relax the body and reverse the stress response. This includes training the mind to modify physiological responses that are generally automatic. For example, focusing on warming hands or feet through thinking has been used as an automatic exercise.

Autogenic training can be used to minimize or reverse the stress response and can be very effective. However, when you learn from a professional it works better and requires time and effort. Unlike breathing exercises, you do not easily learn a few minutes. Autogenic training requires an extra initial effort, but it is capable of quickly and easily amplifying your stress using your mind. You can also learn to control other body systems if you like.

Find support

Having a supportive friend to lose weight in times of stress can be a relief. In fact, in those moments, especially in women, there is a "tenderness and friendly" response that makes us look for support, which is helpful for surviving stressors, for us as individuals and as members of a group

Long meetings with a good friend or therapist can be very helpful for distress. However, quick talk from a close friend can be an easier way to get to a place where you feel more relaxed, and you can consider your stress relief technique. Studies show that taking this support can lower cortisol levels, the stress hormone in the bloodstream, a standard indicator of stress and make people less distressed.

The important thing to keep in mind is to return everything you receive from any relationship. Make sure you match well with the friends you rely on, so don't ask for more than you feel comfortable with. And be sure to be there if you need support. Effective ways to calm down quickly are important, but monitoring long-term relationships is also important.

Tips to Get Started

Finding relaxation techniques that work for you can provide you with a quick way to reverse your stress response and relieve stress management from a more powerful place. In addition, these techniques work quickly within minutes and require little practice before offering at least some effective stress relief. If you can quickly minimize your stress and get more motivation when using these techniques, you may be more successful with the techniques you will read later in this book.

Here are some simple ways to get started right now with the relaxation techniques mentioned in this chapter:

— Try a different technique every day. You may find that you like to try every technique while reading about it. While this is definitely a possibility, you may not have time to try each at this time. If you show

Different techniques every day during the week or about a week may make this process easier. You can also see how each one helps you relieve stress in the real situation you are using. (Relaxing breathing exercise while reading and reading a book may be different from practicing breaks in the office.)

Using different strategies within the identical conditions over the direction of per week might also come up with a real idea of what to do. It is better for you in this situation.

This is a simple way to compare and contrast them.

— Try each one for a week. Following the same technique for a week can help you improve, making each technique more natural and practical. This strategy also gives you a better chance to see how these techniques work over time. Immersing yourself in a single, flourishing habit (rather than trying a number of different techniques over a short period of time) lets you get in touch with that habit: Get in the habit of feeling faster and automatically Relax.

Changing a different habit after a week allows you to try several things before you are tied to any of them that you no longer want to try, but still give you a real idea of Learn how each technique works to help you relieve stress if used constantly.

Keep your memories to see what's best. One of the handiest ways to create a new habit is to hold a diary round it. To make an analogy, people trying to spend much less cash can first discover what they are presently spending and what they are doing and then finding methods to lessen what they are buying, based totally on their unique valuation of in which their money goes and appearance wherein it's far wasted.

Journaling can still be useful because the costs are recorded in the future: Writing everything you spend on can be a good motivating factor to help you spend less, just to avoid accepting it in black and white.

Writing a diary can help in a similar way to relieving stress. You can record the time of day when you feel stressed, which can help you remember when using your techniques. You can record how each technique works, which facilitates comparison and contrast. Finally, you can use them several times, which may remind you and reinforce this habit. The path to journaling requires little effort, but it can reward you in terms of helping you better assess when you need stress relief and the best way to do it.

Restructure and Balance Your Life

If you have not discovered it yet, your brain is not separated from your body and not from your environment. It means that what you put in your body, do with your body and surround it in your life, affects how you feel, how you think, how you perceive your world, enough or not enough. No, and finally how you react. A balanced life means that you are more balanced.

You may be thinking, "Is life balanced? I don't have time for that! If I had time to be balanced, I wouldn't read this book!"

And you can be absolutely right. By saying this, you can always balance your life, even if you don't have time.

This may additionally imply making a few adjustments over a time frame that needs to govern the pressure reaction in every way possible in order that it does now not get irritated easily. Keep in thoughts that the more you misuse your lifestyle habits, the greater you'll see the world, take matters individually and sense more careworn.

For example, I understand that after I eat meals high in processed sugar or excessive in sugar, I sense anxious and tense the following day. I have much less patience, I am greater irritable and my negative memories play an extra prominent role in my mind. Then it is enough to sleep.

Have you finished the questionnaire? What parts of your existence or infrastructure do you need help with? In this chapter, I will overview what I assume are critical elements of the infrastructure that can help maintain the peace, sense higher and find more happiness.

Nutrition to Make You Happiness

The sentence "You have heard what you consume." It's very true. If you eat bad, you may get broken. If you eat healthful and nutritious meals, you'll experience the identical. In what state do you watch you are greater vulnerable to stress?

Your mind works 24 hours an afternoon, 7 days every week and you need excessive nice energy, largely from the meals you devour. The energy you take in has a wonderful effect on the structure and function of your mind and temper. Like an expensive machine, your mind is pleasant served with premium fat that come from meals that incorporate vitamins, minerals, antioxidants, proteins, complicated carbohydrates and good fat that feed the mind. It slows down and protects it from harm.

When you devour more than premium gas, your brain suffers. Low-satisfactory fuels such as refined sugars, trans fats, processed foods and chemical compounds can harm the mind because they reason inflammation, have negative results on insulin and purpose oxidative stress, which is within the technique of oxidation.

Science now shows us that a weight loss plan containing subtle sugars can worsen temper disorders, including melancholy.

One of the reasons why this happens is because a poor diet reduces serotonin levels. Serotonin is a neurotransmitter that helps regulate sleep, appetite, pain and mood. About 95 percent of serotonin is produced in the intestine, which is covered by millions of nerve cells that connect directly to the brain.

In the lining of your intestine, it also has friendly bacteria that help digest and absorb nutrients, protect against toxins and inflammation, and affect the production of neurotransmitters such as serotonin.

When you eat a small amount of food, such as a regular western diet, you not only eat foods that do not contain the nutrients needed to build neurotransmitters and burn your brain, but you also eat foods that cause inflammation. It becomes "rust." Good bacteria and more stress in your body The higher the stress, the greater the stress hormone, cortisol, which can lower the levels of vitamins and minerals absorbed, including B vitamins, which usually have a positive mood. Affections as the inflammation spreads to your body and the necessary vitamins and neurotransmitters are destroyed, so does your mood.

I encourage you to keep in mind that eating different foods will make you feel not only at the moment but the next day. Your diet, in vain and unintentionally, detects your brain. Even if you can eat comfortably when you go down, many of the foods you choose are not good for your brain and, therefore, will help you little by little, not for your health or your mood. The best way to get real attention is to keep your diet high or low with your mental changes.

The key to feeding your mood is to keep a newspaper. Avoid refined sugar (especially high-fructose corn syrup), processed foods and white flour products. Avoid fried foods and foods rich in hydrogenated oils and trans fats. Eat lots of vegetables, two slices of fruit, lean and hormone-free proteins daily, a few nuts and seeds, and healthy fats, keeping your grains to the lowest as possible. Also, try to stick to the 80/20 rule— Eighty percent clean and 20 percent whatever you want, always keeping track of how different foods may affect your mood.

Move It or Lose It: Exercise

I cannot emphasize enough how important exercise and movement is to maintain balance. Note that the man was not destined to be sedentary. We toured the land, seeking refuge, stealing food and building castles. The term "survival of the fittest" should tell you that a couch potato does not work for the survival of the species. Being sedentary is also not conducive to maintaining a happy mood.

Not only does exercise offer numerous health benefits, it also helps control the stress response and helps increase serotonin and endorphin levels, which increase mood. For example, exercising when you are angry gives you the opportunity to release empty energy and have the opportunity to think.

In general, keep track of your daily activities. You may consider getting a Fitbit or other type of monitor that shows the impact of your efforts on your pulse, breathing and sleep.

Have fun or you will get bored and stop exercising. Find friends or a sports friend who can help you overcome your problems. Exercise while outdoors.

Find Social Support

As social beings, humans want to be in the group because our support for our health and well-being is very important. Due to the release of oxytocin and the depletion of the stress hormone, social support helps us feel better, more capable and healthy, especially if relationships are strong and loving.

The keywords here are "strong and loving" because when love is strong between you and others, it sustains you and gives your life, reason and meaning. It reminds you that you are valuable and valuable, and it helps you keep peace and yourself in peace. This love makes you feel more secure and protected. It stimulates your growth and personal identity and helps you manage life's problems, ultimately controlling your response to stress and your morals.

For most of you who have a distress switch and often turn on, you might lack so much love in your life. In fact, it may be the reason why you feel so tense at times that the relationships in your life are not comprehensive or loving enough, or at least you don't understand them that way. If you are in relationships that are not your friend, supporter or supporter, as you receive it, you will be in constant distress. That is, lack of love, that's why you feel bad in the first place.

So, when evaluating the social support section of your infrastructure, you want to analyze how good supporters are in your life and how good it is to get support. If you can't ask for help and get help, the problem may not be someone else's, but it's not about your ability to love or know how to ask.

Understand how you feel (more hours of sleep, healthy food, intimate conversation, the person who really listens to you, hugs, etc.). When it comes to what you may need at any given time, choose the right people who can help you with those needs (don't go to car mechanics to repair your broken leg).

Practice asking for help. Practice so that people know that sometimes you just want to be heard, not what is said. Be sure to contact a friend or friend every day, by phone or in person. You may want to agree with them when the check will take place.

Play at least once a week at least once a week with the person you know best or the relationship you want to cultivate. Join a club, support group, spiritual / religious group or community that shares your interests.

Finding Oneness: Spirituality

Feeling that you belong is not just about finding people near you, but about connecting with something bigger than you or connecting with your spirituality. Being spiritual does not mean being religious, believing in

God or even praying. It is about sharing, giving and receiving love for what is beyond you, what you see and what is in front of you. It is about faith.

Faith enables you overcome hard situations, realize that you aren't alone and find meaning. The greater which means it has in lifestyles, you'll sense helpless in adverse conditions and, in general, you'll experience more valuable. Although I am no longer a fan of religiosity, I suggest that if there is anything you experience you need to agree with in (a selected spiritual or spiritual belief, method, nature or purpose), take the time to get concerned in it. It let you build faith in something bigger.

An easy way to start is to communicate regularly with a sense of fear.

You can do it by admiring a beautiful sunset or other aspect of nature and making a concerted effort to see the little miracles around you. You can also create a meditation exercise that reduces your stress response and gives you access to happy chemicals that will make you feel at ease.

Your meditation practice does not need to sit in the lotus position and sing "ohm" for hours and hours. There are many different techniques you can try, including conscious meditation, yoga, tai chi, progressive muscle relaxation, guided meditation, mantra meditation, conscious walking in nature and more. The key is to create a sacred and quiet place to sit, walk or lie where you can rest (but not sleep), find an approach to focus on, such as an image, word, prayer, phrase, object Beauty and fear (such as nature) or movement: assume illegal behavior and let your daily thoughts go away.

You can join a church, synagogue, Buddhist temple or any other religious or spiritual community with which it resonates. Create a daily ritual of prayer and thanksgiving at the beginning of the day, dinner or bedtime.

Close five to twenty minutes a day to close your eyes and breathe deeply because you are thinking of an impressive experience. Keep a miraculous magazine, where you keep the day you feel grateful for your life and the little miracles you witness.

Develop a meditation exercise (you will get advice on this book). Spend more time in nature.

Choose Nature over Screen-Time

As a community, we become addicted to screens. Using the information highway on a smartphone or computer can help with exercise, meaningful social interaction, healthy eating and adequate sleep. The researchers found that there was a strong association between time in front of the screen and the highest rates of depression, anxiety, poor performance and empathy. 8 What this means to translate is more stress, less patience and average people.

If you want to stay as one of the statistics, go to the right and be miserable. But if you want to find happiness, you can turn off the screen and return to nature. In fact, science now shows us that nature reduces stress hormones and improves our immune system.

Twenty minutes is just what you need, but the better, the better. Work in the garden, stroll through the park, visit the ocean or relax while lying on the ground after a picnic. Make your choice It is important to spend time in nature, feel nature, see nature, eat nature and yes, smell nature. If you do, you will feel less anxious. It is also a spiritual activity, so I encourage you to mark your experiences in nature in your daily activities and moods.

In essence, you want to immerse yourself in the experience of your nature and all your senses. Smell, feel, taste, listen, look and enjoy the wonders that surround you. In addition to keeping your mind away from the stress of the day, you are exposed to nature's healing chemicals called phytoncides, chemicals that reach your brain through the nose that stimulate or relax your brain, and may even leave the system. Your immune system also benefits because it reduces stress. Answer 10. In summary, immersing yourself in nature helps your brain to become a positive state of mind, turn off the stress response and connect more spiritually.

Get Enough Sleep

Lack of sleep has negative consequences in almost every aspect of your health and life. It damages your immune system, hormones, muscle and bone mass, brain function, heart and weight. Did you know that studies show that people who sleep less than six hours a day have a higher risk of becoming obese than people who sleep seven to nine hours? 11 This may not seem like much to you, but there is the inability to lose weight. A great reason why many of my patients are upset. If you are like these patients, you will be disappointed when the scale does not change or increase. You get angry at your body and yourself and you shorten with people close to you. You feel worse about yourself and you fill your face because lack of sleep makes your food cravings soar.

Sleeping more than seven and a half hours can stop this cycle, even if you don't do it all at once, or with the accumulation of naps and eyes throughout the day. The question is, why don't you get enough sleep? Is your partner snoring? Do you snore? If you snore loudly and sometimes you wake up snoring, you may have sleep apnea, which occurs when the airways are blocked. This can be a serious condition, therefore, consult your doctor, who can give you treatment. Worth it Trust me

What other reasons could they be? Do you find it difficult to sleep or sleep? How much caffeine do you drink? Do you get a lot of stimulation at night with electronics, work or television? Do you have difficulty wrapping?

You don't have to experience your life in a private and angry dream, so it forces you to evaluate your dream with your mood and compare it with other reports. You may notice that when you eat, exercise and communicate with spirituality, you sleep better. In the comments section, write notes that may have affected your sleep or the symptoms you have experienced. For example, you could write about food cravings, if you feel more stressed, struggling with sleep and other physical complaints.

Try meditation before bedtime or other relaxation techniques, such as progressive muscle relaxation: start with the soles of the foot and move toward your head, press each muscle group for five seconds, and then allow those muscles to rest for 30 seconds.

Do not leave electronic devices in the bedroom, especially at work or anything that stimulates your brain. Use your bed only for sleeping or having sex. Keep the bedroom space quiet, dark and at a comfortable temperature. Avoid liquids after 8 p.m.

Until you awaken to go to the bathroom.

If you continue to feel tired at the same time as slumbering for greater than seven or 8 hours, consult your physician to look a sleep have a look at to ensure you do now not have a few underlying conditions, such as sleep apnea, that can deal with yourself.

While working to rebuild and balance your life, you are likely to feel lighter, happier, more relaxed, more satisfied and, ultimately, less anxious.

Adopt Long-Term Resilience Habits

Some stress reduction techniques, when used repeatedly, can actually provide long-term resistance to stress. This chapter shows the research behind some of these most useful activities and offers clear guidelines for adopting these long-term habits. Use meditation, exercise or journaling, or embrace all three.

Not all stress reduction strategies have the same levels of flexibility. This chapter contains three effective ways to reduce stress. Each of them can learn independently, obtain benefits in minutes and accumulate cumulative benefits over time. Almost everyone practices them. I encourage you to try each one and consider one, two or all three as part of your lifestyle.

Meditation

As you will remember from the previous chapter, this powerful technique has gained popularity in recent years as researchers have discovered significant benefits to reduce stress. In addition to the fundamental short-term benefits of meditation as a stressful reliever, some of which I discussed earlier, when this is done in the long term, this technique conveys additional strengths. Below are some of the benefits you can get from meditation if you practice regularly for more than a few weeks.

There are several types of meditation that can be practiced and all can bring benefits to relieve stress. Any variation can be based on personal preferences and personality traits of different individuals. Some forms of meditation are easier for a certain person than others, and some forms can be attractive at different points of development. In general, meditation techniques are divided into two main types: centralized and decentralized.

Centralized care techniques focus on a focal point. Attention to an object, feeling or idea leads. This feature allows massive changes in focus on meditation. The focal point can be a candle, a mantra, a piece of chocolate or the sound of one's breath.

Decentralized meditation, also known as mindfulness meditation, takes a more holistic approach. Instead of paying close attention to a subject, awareness of everything is the central concept of this form of meditation: it can be said that the present moment is the focus. Focused methods are much easier for beginners to learn, but both are effective in managing stress and both types can be easily practiced after learning.

Respiratory meditation

One of the most popular forms of meditation, especially for beginners, is self-meditation. Because our breathing is constant, rhythmic and effortless, the sound and sensation of breathing provide an extremely efficient and effective approach to the practice of meditation. Also, because meditation works best with a physically calmer form of breathing, learning this type of breathing and learning to meditate tend to work together. When the body is stressed, our breathing changes to a more superficial and faster pattern, and a return to a more relaxed pattern can help reverse the response to stress, so relaxed breathing combined with meditation to relieve stress is helpful. in itself. That's right. Here are some easy steps to a simple breathing meditation:

— Find a quiet place to rest and relax.

— Set the alarm for the time you want to practice. (This will allow you to have complete peace of mind and know that you will not miss anything important to do after the meeting, to worry about falling asleep or otherwise amazing.)

— To further adjust your breathing, you may want to count on each breath, such as practicing breathing in key 2, slowly counting up to 5 inhalations and counting on each exhale slowly, 8 breaths, and keeping your breathing at a slow pace. Counting can also give you a few minutes of concentration, which helps you get into a more meditative state, especially if you are a beginner.

— You can stop counting and stop concentrating on changing your breathing when you feel completely relaxed. Instead of changing your breathing patterns at this point, just take care of yourself as you leave the body. As your mind wanders (and inevitably will) think of things other than your breathing, slowly divert your attention to the sound and sensation of your breathing. Do not think about that. Just Do It This is an important part of the training.

— You can continue your alarm until it sounds or you feel your session is over.

This breathing meditation is a simple advice for teaching and learning and makes it a popular meditation for beginners. As stated, this is one of the many styles of meditation that can be of interest to you. The following are a number of the most popular kinds of meditation: a quick description of them:

Mantra meditation

This kind of meditation is very powerful and it is able to be less complicated for a few people to practice other forms. This includes focusing on a particular mantra, which can be anything you choose. (Many people like to choose sounds like om and one, which is simple and uncompromising to repeat; others like to choose words or words that have meaning, such as hope or peace. Any mantra you choose, obviously Depending on you and you can choose according to what resonates with you.) Mantra meditation follows the same basic pattern as breathing meditation, except to repeat the mantra aloud or inside your head. When you repeat it slowly, when you repeat that word (if you repeat it out loud) you focus on the sound of the word and the emotions you feel. As your mind wanders through other thoughts, slowly redirect it to the mantra.

Musical meditation

This type of meditation, listening to music, along with meditation, has significant benefits. Choose music that is relaxing and enjoyable and simply focus on the sound. Let emotions flow in your body and focus on emotions. However, be careful to keep your mind clear and simply focus on the feeling.

Kindness meditation

This meditation, also known as a goal, brings you positive thoughts and feelings and can help you get rid of the anger and hostility you can feel towards others. Instead of focusing on the mantra, it is a meditation on the feeling of love and gratitude. Surround yourself with these positive emotions: Surround yourself with love and light and see if you can feel it in your body. Then, think of anyone who loves and surrounds love. Really feel it in your heart and body. Then go to acquaintances and those you do not know, and those who may feel tired, and eventually those who may be angry or angry. Allow yourself to let go of the negative emotions you may have, since it allows you to have positive and loving emotions that capture your consciousness and surround you with that person. You can direct the kindness meditation to all groups of people and even to other countries. The benefits include reducing anger, negative mood, stress and anxiety, and increasing positive social feelings and hope.

Exercise

Exercise is a highly recommended stress reliever for many reasons. As I discussed in previous chapters, physical activity has many benefits in addition to reducing stress, and these benefits alone (increased health, longevity and happiness) make exercise a worthwhile habit. And as a stress management technique, it is more effective than others. The combined benefits of these two facts make physical exercise a lifestyle that is worth following.

The following types of exercise are highly recommended for stress reduction because they have specific properties that are effective in reducing stress in short and long-term stress management:

Yoga

The gentle stretching and balance of yoga may be what people think when they practice, but there are several other aspects of yoga that help reduce stress and a healthy life. Yoga entails the same type of diaphragmatic breathing this is used with meditation. In fact, a few yoga styles include meditation as part of their practice (in fact, most types of yoga can take you to some degree of meditation).

Yoga also includes balance, coordination, stretching and styles are the exercise of power. All support health and stress reduction. Yoga can be practiced in many ways. Some yoga styles feel like a gentle massage from the inside, while others sweat and hurt you the next day, so there is a yoga school that can work for most people, even for those who have some physical limitations, to be attractive.

Walking

Walking is one of the easiest medications to relieve stress that is excellent because of the benefits this technique offers. The human body was designed to travel long distances, and this activity generally did not cause as much wear as it did. Walking is an exercise that can be easily separated by the speed you use, the weights you carry, the music you listen to and the location and the company you choose.

This type of exercise can also be easily divided into 10 minutes of sessions and classes are not needed and no special equipment is needed beyond a good pair of shoes. (This is an advantage, since studies have shown that three 10-minute workouts provide the same benefits as a 30-minute session: great news for those who, due to their busy schedule, need to practice in parts! To find the More smalls!)

Martial Arts

There are many forms of martial arts, and although each one may have little focus, ideology or set of techniques, they all have benefits to relieve stress. These practices tend to pack both aerobic and strength training, as well as the confidence that comes from physical and self-defense skills.

Generally practiced in groups, martial arts can also offer some of the benefits of social support, as classmates encourage each other and maintain a sense of group interaction. Many martial arts styles provide philosophical views that promote stress management and peaceful life, which you can choose or not accept. However, some styles, especially those with high levels of physical combat, have a higher risk of injury, so martial arts are not for everyone, or at least not all styles work for everyone. If you try several different martial arts programs and talk to your doctor before following the style, you have a better chance of finding a new habit that keeps you fit for decades.

These three examples are not the only types of exercise. They simply show some benefits and are usable by most people. There are many other forms of workout that can be very powerful, such as Pilates, running, weight training, swimming, dancing and prepared sports.

Everyone brings their stress management benefits to the table, so discover and practice the form of exercise that appeals to you the most.

Journaling

The two previous strategies have numerous benefits for managing stress and overall health. Although journaling clearly does not offer the same physical benefits as exercise or the same level of relaxation as meditation, it has positive consequences for the body and mind, effects that grow over time. It is also a flexible and accessible operation, so it is worth entering here.

Journaling can make certain emotional changes (based on the intentions of its practice), which can lead to severe stress relief. This can be done in different ways and takes 5 minutes or an hour, depending on the time and goals you may have. If you feel you don't have time to do a meditation or complete exercise at this time, journaling is definitely something to consider.

As a way to reduce stress, journaling brings the broadest benefits expected. It can reduce the symptoms of a variety of health conditions, such as asthma, arthritis and chronic pain. This improves cognitive function. Strengthens the immune system and prevents other health problems. This can help the forgiveness process. In fact, gratitude journaling has shown that it reduces depression over a period of three weeks and journaling generally relieves stress.

Depending on your needs, your journaling practice can take the form you want. You can save a long document on your computer that contains publications related to each day, write a beautiful rainbow font, write your thoughts in a set of articles, Write them in the steam inside you. Bathroom mirrors, or one of the hosts. Find different options. (My journaling has done all these forms over the years and more).

However, some writing techniques are particularly effective in achieving specific objectives. Below are some different journaling techniques that seem to have the greatest impact on stress reduction. Regardless of how you record your thoughts (digitally, in multicolored ink or in steam tracking), these focus areas can be useful.

Journaling focused on emotion: we all have our own problems that cause stress. Exploring feelings of stress and exploring the events behind our emotions can allow us to go beyond our anxiety and anxiety and become a place for inner peace.

Solution-centered journaling

Journalistic techniques that reveal emotions can provide emotional freedom and deeper roots in our experiences. Techniques that include discovering solutions to stressors can be effective in facilitating the process of releasing stressful emotions. This is especially the case with feelings of anxiety or gossip, where steps can be taken to overcome this.

Gratitude Journaling

Journaling is recognized elsewhere, but it has many benefits that are repeated here. Gratitude journaling will have a high-quality effect on emotional wellbeing to the quantity that despair can even increase.

Goal-oriented journaling

This type of journaling facilitates you become aware of in which you live and in which you need to be. You can become aware of targets and divide them into smaller steps. Then you may observe your progress. This will make it less difficult so that it will move via the levels of change, offer a place to congratulate yourself to your successes and will let you get as some distance as feasible for your plans. Or wherein you want to exchange them. This is a fun and authentic form of journaling and does not require daily writing.

Getting started with journaling

The journalistic habit is easy to maintain, although like any new habit, there are things to keep in mind. This habit does not work if you don't really practice it, especially with gratitude journaling; Shorter entries on a regular basis may benefit more from longer entries that seem to work. Rarely written. Also, remember that you can practice journaling at any time, so if you haven't written in your magazine for weeks, you can always back it up and keep writing. Here are some things to keep in mind when starting:

— Choose your place. As mentioned earlier, there are many good ways to keep a diary. Some people like the ease of writing their thoughts on the computer, while others enjoy the old feeling of pencil and paper. Sometimes, having a beautiful diary can inspire you to write more information, while for others, a simple book will put less pressure on writing articles that are "deeper" than authentic ones. Think about what will be best for you and your taste. And don't forget that if this is important to you, take steps to ensure your privacy. Journaling generally works when you don't need to censor yourself.

— Choose your style. As you read previous descriptions of journalistic methods: focused emotions, focused solutions and gratitude, you may find that a particular style resonates with you. Or you may discover that different styles of journaling work best for different situations.

When you sense you have got a feeling of cacophony and have trouble dealing with them, you are focused whilst you are hectic. Thank you. You sense sad and unhappy and you need to recognition at the high quality elements of your lifetime. Keep in mind that your desires for journaling, how you need to feel, and the style of journaling will be less difficult to choose.

— Be flexible. If they reject you for a few days, don't surrender. If your put up is dirty (or your writing consists of errors), it's fine. If you are going to write approximately three belongings you are grateful for, and you can best think of, those are two effective things to your life! Do you need to take pics along with your words? Does it Allow yourself to relax and be flexible with your training? This will make this habit easier and more enjoyable.

Questions to ask yourself

— What are my goals with stress management? Should I relieve physical stress, reduce anxiety, relieve mild depression and practice stress relief?

— Which of these solutions is the easiest in my life?

— What benefits can I get with each of these habits?

— How do these long-term habits fit into my lifestyle?

— Who can help me keep track of these?

— What other support do I need in my life?

— (If you have not tried any of these things in the past and have not continued with this habit) The last time I tried to keep this habit, what was in my way? Could things be different this time?
— What can I do to make a difference?

Evaluate Your Answers

Entering a long-term dependency requires commitment. It allows you recognize precisely what you need to do and why. The look for answers allow you to recognize the matters to help you all through the ride and get back on the right track if you get misplaced.

Knowing what you wish to acquire permit you to make the right choice. For example, if you want to clean your mind of stressful thoughts, a daily journalistic addiction will let your method what you have got in thoughts. A workout session let you clear your head and change your consciousness and permit you to reply much less to stress over time. A dependency of meditation can attain the identical purpose, but in a different manner, so understanding your needs and remembering your parameters can help.

When you have a look at your answers, you must preserve in thoughts that to stay motivated. You will see what you want to use to live on track and what to do in case you cheat. In the subsequent chapter, you'll discover greater methods to enforce those responses for your existence.

Melt Your Mood with Meditation

Although you may still believe that stress is "bad," I encourage you to remember that stress is a powerful force that can motivate and empower you. Therefore, stress is not inherently bad, but energy that must be used for positive action.

What is generally bad is not the stress itself, but the action or reaction that results from it. As I explained, the response occurs as a result of a strong emotional stimulus. The secrets to learn how to separate yourself from severe emotions, like a peaceful warrior, so you can use the electricity of pressure to encourage you to move deeper into a hassle and find solutions. Communicate, be more creative and invent new ideas.

How can you become a peaceful warrior when your instincts take you to a great monster?

You learn to be self-centered to keep calm when you are stimulated or in a stressful situation. Focused learning generally means creating some kind of meditation exercise, in which you motivate yourself to free your mind from negative thoughts, train your body muscles to relax, deepen and detach your emotions and living conditions.

Learn More About Meditation

For many of you, the idea of meditation may seem strange and difficult. You may believe that meditation involves sitting in a lotus position and singing "Ohm" for hours and hours. Although doing this allows you to enter a meditative state over time, you don't have to sing or sit like a leader. There are many ways to meditate, and even better, there is no right or wrong in what you choose to do. You just do it or try to do better than yelling at another person or eating ice cream.

When you meditate, your body changes to a physiological response, which is a mirror opposite to the stress response. In 1971, Dr. Herbert Benson studied physiological changes as participants in the Transcendental Meditation study, and described the physiological changes that occurred during his exercise as a "relaxation response." Including (but not limited to) yoga, prayer, conscious meditation, progressive muscle relaxation and self-hypnosis. The common denominator, he said, was that this response shows a state of deep relaxation that is created by focusing on a simple mental stimulus such as a word, phrase or image such as "in peace, tension.", "Or a prayer, like," God is my shepherd ... "

Dr. Benson's research, along with many other studies in the last fifty years worldwide, has shown that getting a relaxed response can reduce heart rate, blood pressure, metabolic rate, respiratory rate and muscle tension. Improve sleep, reduce the need for medications, reduce pain, reduce anxiety and depression, and reduce symptoms associated with PMS.13 The list is endless.

What is really interesting to me is how this response affects the brain. For example, EEG studies show that people who practice the relaxation response show a slower synchronization of alpha and theta brain waves. Alpha waves are associated with the state of silent awakening, allowing you to be creative and open to new concepts. When you meditate, alpha wave synchronization occurs, which means your ability to be creative, think clearly and get new ideas. The opposite occurs with emotional stress: alpha waves are blocked. Theta activity is often accompanied by a process that connects the upper centers of your brain, such as the cortex and the hypothalamus, mature thinking and emotional processing, deep understanding and alignment with your intuition. Theta waves are also blocked when they are under pressure.

The point is that the calmer and calmer your mind and body are, the more you have access to your intelligence and intuition. In this case, he makes better decisions, finds better words to express himself, and is more creative in finding the right solutions. In addition, in this case, you care without worry. In other words, he loses his emotional attachment to any particular situation and can see it with a separate openness and compassion.

You can see for yourself how pressure and rest have an effect on your capacity to assume genuinely by way of doing the subsequent physical games.

Stress Assessment

Think of a person or situation that you are indignant or disappointed about. Really permit the anxiety in your body and brain increase. Let your self be indignant. Think approximately the character or situation, ask yourself those questions, and write your answers. Try not to over-assume your solutions and write freely instead. Let the words float on the paper.

— What do I need to do with this man or woman or situation?

— Do I experience there may be a solution?

— Do I experience manage or lack of control?

— How would she reply if I had to call or maybe name her at this time?

— What do I do with my breath?

— How does my frame experience? Where do I keep this anxiety?

When examining thoughts, reactions, respiratory, and strain in the body, hold in mind that you can experience uncontrolled or out of control. Did you notice which you held your breath or took a deep breath? Whether you're out of control or now not simply breathing, you ship messages in your brain which are below risk and cause your strain reaction.

To deliver this home, I need to do the subsequent exercising that suggests you how your bodily pressure impacts your intellectual kingdom and the way your mental stress impacts your bodily condition.

Physical Stress Causes Mental Stress

Keep thinking about someone or scenario which you are indignant or disappointed about. As you do, near your fists and blow as if you have been hitting someone.

— Draw a fist firmly on your anger, stick to the other fist and convey both fists together as in case you have been about to attack someone.

— Now try to think about a solution.

— Write down what comes to your mind and the tension to your body.

Can you observe clearly? Describe your experience.

You may discover that you feel better after hitting the air (or the man or woman), but you are probably higher off feeling less harassed and unharmed. You can without difficulty get out of strain using your breath.

Change the Tension with the Breath of Power

Resume your anger and keep pushing your fists tight. Now divert your attention away from anger and focus on your breathing.

— Inhale slowly and count 1-2-3-4.

— Exhale slowly and remove all air from your lungs, count 1-2-3-4-5.

— Do it again. Inhale to four and exhale count to five.

— In the third breath, imagine that all the thoughts in your head are floating in the river, the wind, or the stars.

— Inhale, count to four.

— Exhale, count to five, let all your thoughts and stress flow from your mind and body downstream, to the wind or the stars.

— Inhale, count to four.

— Exhale, in five numbers, let all your thoughts and stress flow.

— Inhale, count to four, and breathe peace and love.

— Exhale, in five numbers, empty your mind and calm your body.

— Inhale, count to four, and breathe peace and love.

— Exhale, in five numbers, empty your mind and calm your body.

Now take a few minutes to notice how you feel, either in the body or in the situation. Do you feel different? Do you care so much? Is there a possible solution? Write freely that thoughts and realities arise.

You can practice this breathing cycle as long as you want, depending on the amount of relaxation and comfort you have over time. Just like holding your breath causes a fire stress response, you decide to take deeper and longer breaths, sending messages to your brain to slow down and relax. By slowing down and relaxing, you get access to the upper centers of the brain and a positive thinking ability, which will ultimately help you regain control of your emotions and actions. That is why I call this breath time the "breath of power." They are souls that give it their power and even control it, even in case of anguish, as you will notice in the next exercise.

Refocus On Breathing

When you are ready, think again of the person or situation. However, hold your breath this time, slowly count four while breathing and count to five while breathing. Ask yourself these questions below:

— What do I need to do for this man or woman or situation?

— Do I experience that there is a solution?

— Do I feel controlled or uncontrollable?

— How do I answer if I was going to pick up the phone and call that person or even call him right now?

— Record your thoughts and observations.

If you practice this breathing cycle for ten to twenty minutes, you will get more peace of mind. If he practiced this meditation every day for ten to twenty minutes, his entire body and mind would become more resistant to stress, which would allow him to remain calm most of the time and have a strong sense of control. Have more information about your emotions and reactions. Using personal care or other meditation techniques will help you overcome your negative points, calm your mind, seek a more positive physiological response and, finally, respond better, even under pressure.

The important thing is to make the sound of its internal negative sound: the one that goes through the stories of its past victimization. Someone who feels control and invisible. Someone who forgets that you are really strong, valuable and loved.

How to Make the Shift?

You have already practiced a breathing exercise that helps calm the mind and calm the body. In most cases, meditation can be simple. The first step is to make the decision to trade your focus from negative questioning to something else: self, word, phrase, sentence, sound, object or movement. By focusing on a particular approach and without judging, repeatedly, over a period of time, you can eliminate the talk in your mind, allowing the stress response to reach your body with muscle. There are many techniques to practice, but I know that using autofocus, progressive muscle relaxation or guided imagery is the easiest way to start.

Progressive Muscle Relaxation

A very effective way to reduce stress is to create stress, believe it or not. The Progressive Muscle Relaxation technique (PMR) involves first tightening a particular muscle group consisting of the forehead or neck for a few seconds and then allowing the equal cycles to relax about thirty seconds later. How your muscular tissues sense while you relax?

You can start from the muscle groups above the head and move towards the soles of the feet or from the feet to the head.

PMR is a wonderful way to reduce stress and anxiety, especially if you practice it frequently. This will help you know which different muscles in your body feel tense and relaxed. When you feel more aware, you can experience this quiet moment when the tension begins. I also like to imagine that the stiffness of your muscles reflects the mental process and stress. This means that the more you practice, the more stressful it will be for you to relieve stress.

PMR practice

To practice PMR, I recommend finding a quiet place to sit where you can rest without sleeping. Although this is a great exercise to be in bed and not able to sleep, your goal is to relax, not sleep, to use this technique in times of stress.

When ready, close your eyes and take five breaths of power. So ...

— Concentrate on your right foot and simply press the muscle of your right foot (bending your toes) hard enough to feel uncomfortable for about 5 seconds but not painful.

— Now let all the muscles relax while all the tension flows from the muscles to the floor. When pulling two, three or more of the respiratory muscles of your right foot (take between fifteen and thirty seconds).

— Move the right foot and the proper foot and squeeze the calf muscle mass for approximately 5 seconds by means of lifting the ft.

— Relax the muscle groups of the proper leg and the right leg and study the tensions which might be released and go with the flow to the ground, even as, 3 or extra breaths carry it.

— Move your whole proper foot and squeeze your thighs, calves and ft. as tough as you can for approximately five seconds.

— Relax the muscular tissues of the proper leg and study that stress is launched and flows to the ground even as respiration, three or greater.

— Do precisely the same with the left foot, the left foot and the complete left foot.

— Drag the movement to the right, urgent the fist as difficult as you could for about 5 seconds.

— Relax your hand muscle tissues and examine that strain is released and flows to the floor at the same time as breathing two, 3 or extra.

— Move on your complete proper arm, push as difficult as you can and squeeze your forearm by pulling your forearm towards your shoulder and building muscle at the same time as clenching your fist for 5 seconds.

— Relax all the muscle groups of the proper arm and observe the tension that is launched and flows to the floor, at the same time as two, 3 or extra breaths carry it.

— Do precisely the equal with the left hand and the whole left arm.

— Move toward the hips and stretch the hamstrings as hard as you can for approximately 5 seconds.

— Relax your hip muscular tissues and take a look at that pressure is launched and flows to the ground due to the fact you breathe two, three or greater.

— Move in your stomach and squeeze your belly as difficult as you can for about five seconds.

— Relax your abdominal muscle mass and take a look at that anxiety is launched and flows to the floor, as it requires two, three or extra breaths.

— Move in your chest, take a deep breath and preserve your chest muscle tissue for about five seconds.

— Relax your chest muscle tissues and have a look at that strain is released and flows to the floor as it requires two, 3 or extra breaths.

— Draw movements inside the neck and shoulders, compressing the shoulders and shoulders by using elevating the shoulders to the ears and holding them tight for about five seconds.

— Relax your neck and shoulder muscle mass and take a look at the tensions that are released and float to the ground, even as, 3 or more breaths deliver you.

— Move your mouth to your mouth, urgent your mouth muscle mass with a grin as huge as viable, and your jaw muscle groups as tight as you may for about five seconds.

— Relax your mouth muscles and observe that stress is released and flows to the floor, while two, three or more breaths carry it.

— Move your eye to your eye by pressing the eye muscles firmly for approximately five seconds.

— Relax your eye muscles and observe that stress is released and flows to the floor, while two, three or more breaths are taken.

— Move to the forehead and press the muscles of the forehead raising the eyebrows for approximately 5 seconds.

— Relax your forehead muscles and notice the tension and flow to the floor because it requires two, three or more breaths.

If you practice PMR regularly for fifteen minutes, this counts as your meditation exercise for the day, which means that your overall stress level will decrease. As I mentioned, the more you practice, the better you'll learn your body and how the muscles tighten or relax. Then, when you feel stressed, you can mark your muscles to rest, which will relieve your stress.

Guided Imagery

Another very effective way to manage stress is to include guided images, where you use your imagination to capture a place, a person or a time and feel relaxed, relaxed and happy. The purpose of this type of exercise is to help you develop the ability to relax and comfort by compromising all your senses and your imagination. When you imagine, for example, on a white sand beach, when you breathe the sun with the freshness of the air in your lungs, the sun shines on your skin, eliminating your emotions from the daily talk and your body in calm. Being. The more emotions you have when you imagine such a positive experience, the more your mind will believe that you are really there and the further away you will be from your negative emotions, thoughts and tensions.

You can use your imagination to capture a beautiful and happy scene or work with negative emotions such as anger using mental images. For example, you can visualize your anger as a symbol or a subject and imagine that it dissolves in the dust. I often use golden light that shines on the sun (or the sky) that resolves the damage in the dust and fills my heart, mind and body with love and peace.

Like PMR, the more you use guided images on a regular basis, especially for ten minutes or more, the better you can metaphorize with the same images to create relaxation in times of stress. It is better to practice in a quiet place where you feel comfortable and do not bother you easily. Set your phone aside and place a DO DISTURB sign on your door if necessary. You can choose an office, bedroom, parking lot, bathtub or create a meditation space in your home. The more you do now not practice in the course of pressure, the simpler it is going to be to use those pics in a bad mood or stimulation.

Happy Place Visualization

— Close your eyes.

— Consider how you feel. You can rate your severity of negative emotions from zero to ten at that time (ten are very sad, angry, sad, etc., and zero because you have no negative feelings). Pay attention to how your body is; if it feels good.

— Take five or six breaths of strength and decide to release your emotions and thoughts every time you exhale.

— Transfer your thoughts and ideas to something positive. Imagine, for example, in your favorite place in nature: maybe relax on a beach, walk in a forest, walk in the mountains, lie on a solarium, work in your garden, watch the sunset from a boat or at Sun. A place where you are always happy and relaxed

— Pay attention to all the details: how do you feel? How are you? What are you wearing? Who is with you? How does the air feel on your skin? What colors do you like: bruises, sky colors at dawn, rosy cheeks of someone you love? What do you hear: waves on the beach against the beach, birds singing or leaves moving with the breeze? Do you taste or smell something: salt on your lips, chocolate or wood aroma in the fireplace? The more details you get and the more senses you have, the better it will be because you keep your focus on the direction of your negative thinking and anger.

— Wherever you are, imagine that you will be happy, relaxed and smiling. Try to stay with these images and explore all your senses for at least 5 to 10 minutes.

— Notice how you feel now, rate your negative emotional intensity from zero to ten.

— If you feel relaxed and do five or six breathing exercises when you are ready.

— Remember that you can go to this wonderful place at any time. This is your way.

— Open your eyes now.

As I mentioned, when you calm the mind, relax the body and breathe for a long time, you meditate. When you add visual images that not only relax, but also relieve stress and negative beliefs, you can improve on a deeper level. You can use images to discover your negative emotions and where they originated, and imagine new situations that resolve negative emotions. Also, when you combine peaceful and charming visual images with physical exercises, such as PMR, you can train your mind and body to relate some of the peaceful images to muscle relaxation. Again, the more you practice this technique, the more your body will learn to move it to release it and relax.

Meditation Combo

Whether you decide to be upset for a few minutes or as part of your meditation training, you will benefit because you combine PMR with images in a way that can help you resolve your stress. And find happiness.

— Close your eyes.

— Observe how you feel and evaluate the intensity of your negative emotions.

— Do five or six powerful breathing exercises.

— Imagine the sun shining on you, golden rays of healing light full of love and wisdom.

— Squeeze your forehead and press your forehead muscles as high as possible, then hold your breath for about five seconds.

— When you imagine the golden light shining on your head, exhale slowly and now move your forehead down, making the forehead muscles relax and release all tension.

— Tense your mouth, squeeze your jaw muscles, smile as much as possible and then hold your breath for about five seconds.

— Exhale slowly when you imagine that the golden light shines through your facial muscles and releases all tension.

— Squeeze your neck and shoulders and press your shoulder against your ear, then hold your breath for about five seconds.

— As you exhale the golden light that shines through your neck and shoulders, exhale and relax slowly and release all tension.

— Squeeze the chest and abdomen, squeeze the abdominal muscles and hold your breath for about five seconds.

— Relax and release all tension when you imagine the golden light shining through your chest and abdominal muscles.

— Squeeze your hips, squeeze your hip muscles and hold your breath for about five seconds.

— Exhale slowly and release all tension when you imagine the golden light that shines through your hips.

— Squeeze your arms and hands and your fist while flexing your muscles, then hold your breath for about five seconds.

— Exhale slowly when you imagine that the golden light shines through it

— The muscles in both the arm and the hand relax while releasing all tension.

— Squeeze your legs and feet, squeeze your thighs and rotate your fingers under it and hold your breath for about five seconds.

— Exhale slowly when you think of the golden light that shines through the leg muscles and relieves all tension.

— You are surrounded by golden light.

— Five or more powers to breathe.

— Consider how you feel.

Keep in mind that there is no right way to meditate. There is only one way to relax and feel relaxed. The more you practice, the better. Don't judge or worry if your mind focuses while you want. Just notice that your mind is active, imagine your thoughts floating and refocusing. Practice, practice, practice. Try yoga, tai chi, transcendental meditation, Buddhist meditation and more. You never know, you could become your Zen master someday! Enter the next chapter to learn more about mental meditation.

Redirect Stress for Good

Like a strong wind, stress can be a powerful force that can drive radial developments, a new direction, defend justice and civil rights, and support those you appreciate. This allows strangers to gather to separate among the rubble or fight for a common cause, promote political programs, boost business, end relationships or align.

Or give people the opportunity to be more with what they usually fear. But like tornado winds, the impact of stress, especially when associated with anger, can be devastating if left unchecked. Therefore, if the powerful force of stress or anger is applied within you and is not expressed or moved, the internal energy will be lost or turned off, like a soda container that shakes and finally opens. The key is to learn how to move stress through structure and direction so that its effects can benefit you and others instead of destroying them.

Learning from Our Ancestors

Wisdom traditions such as Traditional Chinese Medicine (TCM), Buddhist philosophy and the Vedic system have pointed out the positive benefits of turning negative emotions into more vibrant and healthy ways for thousands of years. In the five-element TCM system, anger, one of the most destructive negative emotions, is understood as a form of negative energy that is associated with an unbalanced liver, stagnation, explosive growth and causing roots to leave the ground, and a variety of problems Health such as anxiety, hypertension, blood clots and liver disease. When it is positively balanced, energy communicates with kindness and compassion, strength, creativity, speed of action and movement, gentle growth, "branch" sound, green color and spring.

In the Vedic tradition dating from the year 2000 a. C. in India, the chakras system also provides guidance to change anger more positively. Chakras, which means "wheel" or "tornado" in Sanskrit, are vortices of energy and consciousness that revolve like the sun. There are seven main chakras in the body that are interconnected by the spine, each associated with specific organs and physiological, physical, psychological, emotional and spiritual functions, colors, sounds and vibrations.

The chakra most related to anger is the third chakra located in the solar plexus. It is located between the rib and the navel and includes the upper abdomen, stomach, spleen, intestine, liver, pancreas and gallbladder. It is thought that this power middle includes innovative and intuitive skills, in addition to the intellectual side of the mind, soaking up thoughts, breaths and experiences that help you define yourself.

The 3rd healthful chakra represents the healthful digestive tract, in which you realize who you're, what you feed and what you don't, capable of absorb and soak up lifestyles reports in a healthful way without getting misplaced or lost. You can surrender and remove everything that does not serve you, assist you or enhance you. The 1/3 unhealthy chakra is characterized through emotions of insecurity, doubts, shame, guilt, anger, anxiety and a myriad of digestive problems. And kindness with yourself and others.

What Does This Mumbo-Jumbo Mean?

Now he knows that by controlling the stress response, he can control negative emotions, which he can do by creating awareness and mindfulness, using breathing techniques, developing a meditation exercise, communicating with love and staying healthy. Ancient wisdom traditions support the use of these tools not only to control the response to stress, but also to convert the negative energy of stress into loving energy that benefits you and others. The bottom line is that these traditions provide you with more tools that not only reduce your stress, but also direct the energy to the other side with which you can work well. These tools do not include gaining stressful energy to relax and keep you captive so you can focus on your strength and eventually change to love.

Move It to Loosen It

When you consider how your body feels during stress, you feel somewhere in your muscle or body, as if your energy is blocked or stagnant. What do you do with the energy block? You move it The best way to move this energy is to move, be it aerobic exercise or exercise movements performed in yoga, tai chi, qigong or progressive muscle relaxation. This energy can also be "displaced" through music, verbal or body work, such as massage and acupuncture.

Physical Activity

In addition to being beneficial for your long-term physical, mental or physical health, it can help you burn excess energy and release endorphins and other sensible chemicals that help you create a mood. Help you, even when you have it. Consider stress, running, walking, biking, swimming or jumping rope in trouble. You can roll or dance or play basketball, tennis or soccer. Weight training is also a good option. Whatever you choose to do, be careful, since you can be absorbed in your negative thoughts, you can ignore your form and hurt yourself. Personally, I consider that physical activity is a strange release from my anger and despair. I also help in slower movements, such as the mild types of martial arts available in tai chi or qigong or even yoga, while helping to create a sense of calm and tranquility. I call this meditation on the fly.

Shake it Out

— Allow yourself to think of something frustrating or unpleasant. Let the stress increase and pay attention to where you and your body feel restricted or restricted.

— Let your arms and hands sink to your side.

— Begin to twist your legs, following the buttocks, followed by the torso.

— Add your arms and shake them brutally while shaking your head.

— Shake your entire body for a minute, as if you were shaking off all the stress.

— Outside

— Observe how you feel.

Moving Meditation

When you don't have the option of going to the gym or going out for outdoor sports, you always have the ability to do stretching and rest exercises wherever you are. For example, progressive muscle relaxation is a very effective technique that will undoubtedly change the energy of stress, in addition to providing a variety of breathing and yoga techniques. Especially effective are those that involve twisting its core, which means neutralizing the energy blocked in its third chakra. Below are a variety of exercises you can try. Choose one or do them all, one after another.

Supine Twist

— Lie on your back (on a carpet, rug or lawn).

— Push your knees to your chest and hold them in your arms while breathing deeply and as close as possible to your chest.

— When exhaling, allow your knees to move slowly to the left while your head falls to the right.

— Breathe deeply and then, when exhaling, draw the hip with your left hand while the right arm is stretched to the right.

— Relax, breathe, relax, stretch and stretch.

— Do this for ten cycles of breathing on each side.

Kundalini Kriya Pose

— Sit cross-legged on the floor.

— Place your hands on your shoulders and run your fingers over your shoulders.

— Breathe deeply and turn left.

— Turn and turn right and slide the column to the right.

— Keep your eyes closed and twisted twenty-six times.

Alternate Nostril Breathing

— Breathe deeply, then place your thumb in the hole in the right hole and press down when you exit the left nostril.

— Place your index finger next to the left hole and press, raising your thumb, pressing the right nostril and breathing through the right nostril.

— Slide your thumb toward your right nostril and lift your index finger from your left nostril and breathe through your left nostril.

— Do this for twenty-six breath counts.

Sound Therapy

According to ancient traditions, a variety of sounds and prayers can also alter the energy of stress. You can sound these sounds or songs when you pause or make no sound. The following exercises contain some techniques that I use and find useful.

"Shhhh"

According to traditional Chinese medicine, "sand" is a sound that calms the liver.

— Take a hand and make circular movements around your abdomen so that your liver relaxes while breathing and then exhale with the "shhhh" sound.

— Turn your hand around your belly nine times repeating "City."

— Repeat "City" nine times around your abdomen counterclockwise.

Shout "Hello!"

— While sitting or standing, you take a deep breath and exhale, "Hey!"

— Shout at least ten times.

— "Ha!" With movement

— Stand with your feet on your shoulder.

— Raise your arms above your head and breathe deeply. When you leave your arm, pull your arms up, let your head and body follow you (so you bend your neck and slightly your buttocks) while yelling "Hey!"

Sing Out Loud

— Find the song you love and cut it out.

— Sing from the top of your lungs and from the bottom of your abdomen.

— Jump and dance while doing it.

Journaling Stress Out

Writing your thoughts and emotions can be very therapeutic, and I strongly support the use of a stress relief diary, which includes writing reasons that make you feel uncomfortable or stressed with all your emotions without stopping or judging. I do Here is the way I recommend:

Daily stress release

— Set a timer for 15 minutes or keep the time open.

— On a separate sheet of paper from your other diaries, write why you're disillusioned or harassed and what you sense, see, assume or want to do.

— Do not be left behind. Don't think too much about writing without a filter. You can get it.

— You can drag images and use commas or plain adjectives.

— Stop when the timer is turned off or when you feel stuck.

— Put your hands on the words you wrote and say these words out loud: "Now I will free you from my body, mind and conscience."

— Destroy the papers by crushing or crushing them.

— Check with yourself the next day. If you discover that you are still upset or stressed the next day, exercise again.

Focus Your Power

In most cases, it is very difficult to remain silent or silent when you are worried or gossiping about something for which you are upset. Moving helps you release this empty energy so you can strive to be more central, connect with yourself and control your emotions and thoughts. One of the easiest approaches to stay on land is to spend time in nature. Here are 4 easy sports to help you get there. If you do not have get entry to nature, the ultimate 3 sports are in particular useful.

Centering in Nature

The purpose of this exercise is to meditate on the nature of mindfulness so that you can involve all your senses to appreciate everything that surrounds you while using illegal conscience and appreciating the connection you have with nature.

— Take yourself to a place in nature that you love. It can be a forest, an open field, a beach or your garden.

— You can be calm, comfortable, lying down or choose a horticultural position while you are comfortable.

— Close the moment you close your eyes.

— Observe the feeling of air on your face.

— Observe the feeling of air while filling your nose and then your lungs.

— Pay attention to the sounds of nature around you. Is there a bird song? Do the leaves move with the breeze?

— Observe the connection your breath gives to the air, the breeze or the sounds.

— Pay attention to the feeling of the ground under your feet.

— If you kneel, you will feel the ground as you pull it towards your fingers and hands.

— Know the land, this is what farmers are growing.

— Appreciate the land that the land offers you.

— Appreciate being fed by earth, sun, air, rain and anything else that comes to mind.

— Appreciate your place here on earth and your place between heaven and earth.

— Breathe deeply and slowly.

— Now you can start gardening with your mind, walk safely or use all your senses to sit or lie down to appreciate your connection to heaven and earth: listen, listen, Look, feel, taste and taste.

Rooting and Grounding

This exercise is a modified version of a qigong movement (a form of slow and ancient martial arts) that involves moving, balancing and using your imagination to land.

— Stand with your legs over shoulder width, keeping your knees slightly bent.
— Keep your chin upright, pulling the head.
— Close your eyes.
— Take three or four breaths.
— Focus on the soles of your feet and just consider the connection of your feet with the ground.

— Breathe and imagine that you put the energy of the earth on the back of your foot.

— Exhale, open the energy from the front of your foot to the ground.

— Inhale and place the energy on the back of the foot.

— Exhale, open the energy from the front of your foot to the ground.

— Inhale and gather the energy from the floor at the back of your foot and lean back and allow your toes to appear slightly.

— Cool exhalation and energy from the pads of the front feet to the floor, while resting on the pads of the front feet to allow the heels to appear slightly. (Turn a little with each breath and exhale).

— Imagine that the roots form, move deeply into the earth and connect you to the heart of the earth.

— Imagine that the root helps you maintain balance while allowing you to be flexible and relaxed.

— Breathe for at least ten cycles and exhale while inhaling and exhaling while remaining relaxed.

— When ready, get up. Be aware of your connection to the earth and understand how you feel.

Child's Pose

It is a type of yoga that is very relaxing and nutritious. It helps you connect to the ground like a child, let it inhale and exhale slowly.

— Sit on your heels (preferably on a mat, carpet, or soft grass).

— Breathe deeply into your arms.

— While retiring, move forward and place your forehead on the floor.

— Stay for five minutes or more, just breathe.

Liver smile

This is considered one of my favorite recognition exercises that involves making an inner smile for your coronary heart and inner organs, in particular in this version, your liver, even as the use of a sound related to liver balance.

— Stand on a pillow or chair with your ft. flat at the floor, whichever is cushier, and close your eyes.

— Take or three breaths, breathe counting three and breathe whilst counting five, while connecting the bottom of your backbone to the center of the coronary heart and the pinnacle of your scalp to the heart of the world.

— Imagine that the electricity of the earth and the universe connects in your heart while you inhale and exhale.

— Smile slowly.

— Smile while changing your focus and awareness to your heart. Smile in your heart. Smile, breathe and breathe for five more cycles.

— While slowly focusing your awareness on your liver, which is under the right rib cage, breathe deeply, slowly and deeply. Smile with love on your liver. Smile your liver while you inhale and exhale for five cycles.

— Smile in for the next five to ten cycles of breathing and say "show" each time you exhale.

— Sit quietly and discover how you feel.

Shift into Love

You have already learned about the importance of love and its healing powers for health and life, and I hope you enjoyed some of these benefits through meditation. Since love is difficult to achieve in times of stress, it certainly helps move the energy of stress first and then focus on it. Once focused, you can turn negative energy into something positive, using love to do it by evaluating your IMT and seeing what you can do to improve your self-care or get more support.

Take Care

Your assessment of IMT may show that you are irritated because you are irritable due to lack of exercise, sleep, loneliness or irritability. As such, you must first evaluate and update where you need to use love in relation to your attention. You can develop a long-term plan (to sleep, meditate, eat better, etc.) and plan for now. The "new program" may include receiving a massage or healing the body, enjoying a healthy meal, buying your own flowers or taking a nap. Whatever you choose to do, do it kindly.

Social Support

Your TMI evaluation will also show you if you need more help. You want to make sure you have your "Go" people that you can refer to when you need them. These are people you have already identified or want to bring into your life: people who can listen to you, love you or retain you without a trial. You will be surprised how many people can know who can do this for you when you explain what you want them to do. You can go to a support group, a therapist, a counselor or a coach, or get in touch with your friends or loved ones who can remind you how much you love them.

Help Someone Else

A powerful way to redirect and transform relief energy is to use energy to do good, not to harm. Think of a reason why you can believe in him and get involved and use his stress to motivate him to love and help. If there is no specific reason to move it, you can always help anyone who needs it. Get out of your head and emotions and look around. Help an older person cross the street or take their food home. Open the door to people and smile. Volunteer in a soup kitchen. The listing is endless.

The Energy Socket

When you have doubts and are not positive what to do, who to help you with, or even in case you feel the need to move, you could do this exercising to get the affection and aid of the assets that surround you, heaven and manual the earth.

— Stand on a pillow, in a comfortable chair with your ft. flat at the floor or at the ground, and sit down in a snug chair or lie on a soft blanket at the floor.

— Close your eyes and breathe three to four breaths.

If you lie down, connect to the ground, raise your feet, cocaine or your entire back. See how the earth supports it: its weight, its livelihood, etc. Allow yourself to imagine that as you grow from the heart of the earth through your body to your solar lamps, you feed, abundant and love.

— Concentrate your consciousness slowly on the solar plexus when you imagine gathering support, abundance and nutrition for mother earth in your solar lamps.
— When inhaling, accumulate your energy in your body in the bending of the sun.

— When you go out, imagine giving love and generosity to the earth.

— Collect more energy when inhaled.

— Exhale, return to earth.

— Do this for five breathing cycles.

— Relax in your solar particles and inhale and exhale slowly, expanding your power and focus of energy no matter what you experience.

— When you are ready, imagine looking up at the sky and noticing the golden rays of light shining on you.

— When breathing, imagine supporting these golden lights that sustain support, nutrition, abundance and love for the world.

— These rays of light come down from the crown of his head and heart, filling his heart and falling into his solar plexus.

— As you leave, imagine giving the world love and generosity.

— Do this for five breathing cycles.

— As an outlet, you receive heaven, earth, energy, support, food, abundance and love.

— Relax in your solar plexus, inhale and exhale slowly, and notice the sensation you are experiencing, expanding your power and focus of energy while now on earth and earth. Gives.

Putting It All Together: What Redirecting Stress Might Look Like

Here is an example of a stress energy change process:

His boss only got credit for what he has been working for the past two months. He barely mentioned his work, even in his report to the CEO. You say what are you doing

— LEGS: Calm your thoughts and pause for a moment. Recognize that you are angry and recognize how right you feel in doing so. Witness what you feel and the feelings you experience and start labeling the experience (this is a state of disrespect, dishonesty, betrayal, etc.). When labeling experience, separate yourself from emotions and situations and realize that you don't need to get caught in anger.

— Breathe your strength and feel that you are slowly losing your anger.

— Replace the nervous energy of the nose by breathing gently followed by a "Ha!" Do it several times.

— At the end, perform a deeply rooted qigong exercise.

— Stay still for a moment and consider and evaluate your TMI (Trigger, Mood, Infrastructure).

— Change love by practicing energy shots. Make a list of activities you can do to help you feel seen, valued and respected, understand that ignoring or ignoring them is a role model for you, and is somehow creating a situation that you will try to fix.

— Consider how you feel.

Although this process does not alter the outcome of what your boss has done, it will lead you to feel less angry and more empowered, which will ultimately help you direct your reaction and the practical process you can take. Change moment and time. The future Whenever you find an activity or activity that allows you to leave a story, emotion or negative reaction, write it in your anxiety assessment chart to know what you can do in the future.

Always Smile and Let Go

Imagine this: you are capable. You feel safe and open about what life has created for you. You are in the moment and when you look at life and yourself, you realize that this movie is really a movie and you have to choose whether it is a dramatic tragedy or a romantic comedy.

You can also choose if you wait a lifetime for a happy ending or decide to have a happy and lasting journey, realizing that if you are waiting for a happy ending, there is something great in No, nothing will be enough, and you insist that you will be hopeless and Without hope forever, and yes.

I remember that a long time ago when I met a colleague for a business lunch at a nearby restaurant. While we were having a meeting, I was a little distracted because a small child, maybe three years old, began to grimace, not me or anyone in particular, but to experiment with the facial muscles and prove himself. It was entertaining. His mother, who seemed to have a serious conversation with another adult, repeatedly advised him not to eat and take off his face from the cup (he often hid it in his mouth). Then he continued listening to his mother, jumping from his chair and lying on the floor. Every time his face touched the cold ceramic floor, he trembled.

It made me annoy to. Her mother, as much as an adult, was upset, worried about collecting horrible germs and angry because she was behaving because she was not trained. Kudos, who did not shout or raise his voice, shook him silently and put him back in his chair. She didn't cry, but she was completely disappointed. His pancakes were not as interesting as the foam, but the ice contained in his drink! Would my mother do the same if I were a mother? I wondered maybe. I was upset with my son for my son, including myself, and if I fell asleep, worried, anxious or anxious, I was very likely to be angry with my son.

I realized that if I was really present and had a child with curiosity, I would probably want to lie down and put my face on the floor to feel the cold of the tile and see how it was if I had this opportunity, I would probably like a child. I'm three years old. Certainly, my serious sessions would be more palpable, not to mention that shouting would certainly reduce my tensing muscles and probably help a lot in managing my stress.

Why Does Laughter Reduce Stress?

If you think about it, laughter is purely social, and it is part of the human way of life that allows us to unite and go through difficult times. When you laugh, it is rare that others do not laugh at you, since the disease is usually contagious. When people laugh together, their guards go down, self-control goes out the window and a sense of solidarity occurs. When you feel connected and united with others, your sense of belonging and social support improves. Having this support improves your well-being and your ability to deal with problems, strengthen your infrastructure and reduce stress.

Humor and especially laughter are excellent ways to reduce stress. Laughter, for example, stimulates physical stimuli in the body, such as increasing circulating endorphins or happy and happy chemicals. Like progressive muscle rupture, laughter increases the response to stress and muscle tension, followed by relaxation and a decrease in heart rate, respiratory rate and blood pressure. Although studies are inconclusive, laughter can improve your immune system, mood and oxygen and relieve pain. Laughter is a good stress management intervention without complications.

As humans, we naturally put humor in difficult conditions to help us endure the pain of a memory. Think of a situation that happened to you in the past that was very difficult at the time, but now you are telling a funny story. How long did it take you to do that with that special memory? Is there any memory you can't easily find in your wits?

The deeper the wound, the more it will hurt and probably serve as a trigger for your anguish. When you include humor in the equation, the lens of how you view memory changes. You make it a little brighter and it offers you a more open perspective that allows you to see the situation more objectively. In short, humor and laughter help you release your attachment to negative memories and beliefs, turn off your stress response, connect with a happier mood and, therefore, have happier memories and ultimately, painful situations or stress. Better management

Evaluation with humor

Step 1: Return your thoughts to a time when you felt humiliated, humiliated or embarrassed by someone else's actions. Allow yourself to experience the pain without feeling comfortable. Just do what you have learned, observe the physical response of the body and the emotions that follow.

— Do you feel contracted or expanding?

— How do you rate your emotions?

— What about the humiliating situation?

— How does it make you feel about yourself?

— How do you feel or feel about the person or people who made this possible?

— Record your thoughts, answers and observations.

Step 2: Implement PAWS.

— Breathe deeply and exhale completely.

— Exercise self-esteem when entering and leaving.

— Watch the chest as it goes up and down.

— Be as you feel when inhaling and exhaling.

— Separate from experience practicing awareness of the present moment.

Step 3: allow yourself to step back so you can take a look

- Live it as if you were watching a comedy with the main characters.
- And issue support
- Watch the movie and see which scenes are or can be fun.
- Will this be a slapstick comedy if someone falls or falls?
- Maybe this movie is like Woody Allen, where this comedy is accompanied by subtle words and delicacies?
- Write a new story.

Studies have shown that humor is an optimal solution to deal with negative situations, especially when reevaluating subsequent memories, as it helps people deal with negative stimuli without collecting or minimizing their memory. To find a better one.

Therefore, it allows you to respect your memory, emotions and state, while giving you the opportunity to see a broader perspective without shrinking in your own smaller being and being in a pattern of negative thinking and behavior. The more you can find humor in your life, the better it will be in periodic assessments with humor.

Be Clear and Irresponsible

In my opinion, laughter and ingenuity are more reflected in better coping styles or a better ability to socialize. They are also my options to rejoice and be more childish, open, curious and fun in life than at risk.

Children do not apologize for being themselves. They are simply not suffering from the past or the expectations of the future that is still happening. They still don't care what others think. Due to curious creatures, children want to explore, learn, touch, feel, laugh or snore. Most adults, on the other hand, have lost the game and curiosity of their childhood, and are often afraid or anxious about future expectations based on past experiences or judgments. However, adults have a fully functional mind and the ability to recognize, learn or grow from past experiences and allow them to make wise decisions in the future.

The key is to combine the fun of the work with the wisdom of life without being prey to fear and negativity. I call it lighting.

Turning on means not being serious about yourself and being in the position and enlightenment of your heart, being open-minded and illegal for you.

We were all satisfied to meet the expectations of others and were told to behave in a way that would inevitably occur at the expense of our natural spirit and personality. Most of us have been following the rules and meeting the expectations of others for a long time, we wonder who we really are, we often have difficulty deciding, and if we want something different or insecure if it is inappropriate, we feel selfishness mold.

Entering your power means being outlawed and making you laugh.

You can be irrational, intelligent and a little funny, sometimes crazy or hurt, for being crap, having messy hair, being a person who can throw things or travel wherever you are. Being. You can be ignorant and jealous of your shortcomings.

The more you stay in your power, the more you can accept yourself for who you are: be human, accept your strengths and weaknesses. You can approach this by bringing laughter and humor to your life. The more powerful you are, the more laughs you can connect with your childish state.

Move the Negative Energy with Laughter

There are many options for you to work on your funny bone and bring more humor to your life, even when you are angry. In fact, laughter, especially in the form of yoga, laughter and journaling to joke, is an excellent way to move the energy of stress. I think that using laughter techniques in times of distress is not always easy, but it is easier to do, especially if you have done things to improve yourself and your memories, as explained in previous chapters.

Laughter yoga

Also known as Hasyayoga, Laughing Yoga is a yoga practice that involves quiet breathing, stretching and voluntary laughter. It was started in 1995 by Dr. Madan Kataria, who believed that laughter could have many physical benefits, otherwise, yoga would have to be done in a group, making eye contact and group laughter. Finally, it leads to a true contagious laugh. I don't mean the little words here and there. I mean a big laugh that makes you cry your eyes and your stomach hurts. You know, what catches and generally makes everyone laugh.

The important thing here is that the laughter is done at least, not in others, for at least ten to fifteen minutes. Laughter is a deep and strong laugh that comes from the deepest, so this is a virtual release of dense energy. You can imagine how this type of cathodic could be. You could imagine that while you're really laughing, all your worries and worries go out the window and allow you to be more childish and playful.

Since you may not be able to skip yoga classes when you are stressed, you can practice alone, which I recommend. Why Because the more you laugh, the better you need to laugh at your body (such as ordering the muscles to rest while practicing progressive muscle), and you will be more relaxed and playful. The more relaxed and playful you are, the more likely you are to be humiliated. This exercise usually involves first kicking, then breathing and then laughing.

Solo Laughter Yoga

Step 1: Warm up

— Cover your hands rhythmically and make sure that all parts of the palm and fingers are in full contact.

— While doing this, "Ho, ho, ha, ha, ha!" Repeat at least three times. The mix is believed to stimulate pressure points of medicine and stimulate energy movement, while singing activates the diaphragm and makes the body breathe deeper.

— You can move your hands up and down, or rotate them from side to side, and still follow the sounds with the sound

Step 2: Power of Self

— To ensure inhaling and exhaling through the abdomen, you can draw some powerful breaths, lift your arms and smile while breathing, and lower and relax your arms when you exhale.

Step 3: Activate Laughter: Laughter Slope

— Start smiling.

— Laugh slowly.

— Allow laughter to start laughing. Laugh louder and louder to reach the height of laughter.

— Relax your knee and jerk.

— Slowly reduce that laugh to a laugh.

— Turn off laughter to smile again.

Step Four: Center the laugh and hit the ground

— If you feel for two or three minutes, strengthen your ego and laugh.

— When you are ready, sit quietly with your powerful breaths and let your body go into a state of relaxation and strength until you need it.

Comic Presentation

In the previous chapter, you practice with symbols that allow you to feel more power. You can keep these tips in touch with comedy to help your mood and mood without feeling worse, ashamed or less.

Superman / Superman with Twist

If you feel anger has increased, do the following:

— Suppose you call Superman / Superpower.

— Put a layer on or imagine that you are really wearing a layer.

— Move as if your muscles are swollen and large and your hands are stretched over your hips and legs (without bending your knees).

— Speak aloud about how to use your super powers to beat the talk.

Curse Like a Foreigner

— Stand with your shoulder width apart.

— Raise one arm with the elbow bent and lift your finger toward the sky.

— Curse with foreign accent or pirate accent.

Prank Journaling

When you're upset about something, especially when you realize you're probably exaggerating, sit down and write about things as if it's a clown or a romantic comedy, or if you can, write three or four jokes. For example, when you get back to a dirty house by screaming at the kids, you can go back to the scene. You can write about a scene where you're clinging to something and then you make a displacement attack while simultaneously grabbing a piece of dust and cleaning the room with one hand before landing completely. You do. This is your chance for creativity. Take at least 5 minutes to write and don't think too much. Enjoy the process.

Writing Comic

— Write down details that describe what made you angry.

— Write the words in the story on a different sheet, but this time keep a large gap or spaces between the words.

— Insert sentences, curses or anything else you want, including pictures, between words to create a humorous story.

Centering and Grounding with Joy and Laughter

Laughing yoga practice is a great start to eradication, especially when you allow yourself to visualize it. In addition, you can play in nature or use your imagination.

Mind-building game in nature

— Find a place in nature where you can feel safe and relaxed.

— Practice mindfulness, but do it as if you were a curious child who saw things for the first time.

— Choose branches with a sense of curiosity.

— Lie on the floor and feel the floor below you.

— Smell the flowers, jump and breathe the breeze in your lungs.

If you do not want to go out or find yourself in situations where you cannot stop being childish or have an external expression, you can sit quietly. Doing this exercise will surely make your face smile and make people wonder what you have!

Visualize

— Begin by imagining yourself as a child.

— Watch yourself running, laughing hysterically, you don't care about anything but how funny it is.

— Imagine you are dreaming, jumping, jumping, screaming and snoring: everyone is in your imagination.

— Let your imagination fly and have fun!

The moment you do humor or laugh, you begin the process of directing your stress in a more positive way so that you can better see the conditions of how you feel, label it, and create and activate an expression of power. It is up to you to imagine a power and then walk like a top model or superhero and then curse a foreign language, which certainly allows you to feel more powerful and at the same time light.

You can also use your wits to deflect conflicts or disagreements and reduce stress and anxiety. Keep in mind that if you are really anxious, try to use humor, you may end up making harmful and numb statements because you are simply trying to hide your emotions with humor instead of redirecting them. Do not give up for this reason, you first want to move the energy and concentrate. When you are on the ground, you can use playful humor to open the paths of communication and compassion.

Maintenance of Your Funny Bone

To get used to his sense of humor, especially in difficult times, it is a good idea to work on his honor and preserve his funny bone regularly. If you use it, you will not lose it. In addition, anything you can do to involve your funny bone and help you maintain a positive mental attitude will not only benefit your morals but also your health and relationships. Think about it: the lighter you become, the more serious you become and the more you get angry when life goes wrong.

Here are some activities in which you can participate regularly to improve your sense of humor:

— Look for humor in all the right places: Try to watch a fun movie or TV show at least once a week. You can read comics, go to a comedy club, read a fun book or go to a yoga class.

— Smile whenever you can, for no reason: If you look around, you can find that most people are trapped in their thoughts and rarely smile. Take responsibility for smiling for no reason. You may discover that the world smiles at you. And if they don't, they will wonder what they offer.

— Schedule playback: Plan at least once a week and, if possible, once a day to play. You can do anything to nurture your creativity. You may want to paint, paint, sculpt, puzzle or do some kind of sporting activity for fun. Do what you choose, aim for at least twenty minutes, which will break your brain and help you feel more relaxed and happy later.

— Take time with people who make you laugh and be happy. The more you surround yourself with folks who make you snort and be happy, the greater they remind you that your lifestyles are superb and dull and that you have numerous gratitude for yourself, in particular a laugh and lively friends. Remember, laughter is contagious.

— Keep a thank-you diary: A sure way to fireplace anger is to sense regret and misery. The happier your lifestyles are, the much less likely it is to happen. Take a couple of minutes a day to report three or 4 motives to be kind. Make a list of your blessings.

— Spend time with the children: As adults, we forget how playful we are and how to see the world with a free heart. Take time with the children and observe them. Try to be stupid with them or just chat with them.

— Laugh at yourself: The more you laugh at yourself, the less the lighter side of your paths, without lowering yourself. The more you take seriously, the more easily you will be stimulated.

— Get out: Practice your superhero satire in front of your mirror daily. Walk around the house with your finger in the air and speak with a foreign accent when I tell you about your family's day plans.

Create an Action Plan

You can often get valuable information from books like this, but you are not sure where to start with the ideas. On other occasions, you may not know what ideas to try, or you can make many changes very quickly and eventually reduce the effort altogether. Or it may be good to change the planning, but you have trouble taking your plans to the real level of action.

How to Achieve Your Goals

APRIL

- Make sure your goals are SMART.
- Set milestones.
- Be specific about how to reach goals within a time frame.
- Make your goals actionable.
- Put your actions into a schedule.
- Follow through.

the balance

This chapter provides clear steps for you to create a short and long term stress management plan, a timeline for putting plans in your life and possible strategies for times when you may be experiencing problems.

This book covers many strategies to reduce the stressors in your life and deal with the remaining stressors. It can be hard to recognize wherein those adjustments begin. It can be tempting to make several crucial adjustments at once, or maintain your thoughts approximately what you might want to trade, and in no way take the subsequent step in doing so. As you will remember from the change steps mentioned in the introduction, making lasting changes is not always easy, and having an application in addition to information and ideas will definitely help. At the end of this chapter, you can find a variety of ways to make lasting changes without pressing the process. You can also have a paper design, ready to use.

Why and How to Create a Plan

If you have a plan, stress management will be much easier. Your program can be as simple as "when I despair, take three deep breaths," or it can include a combination of different stress management techniques to use in different situations. I describe stress management programs that are multifaceted enough to cover a variety of challenges, but are simple enough to be implemented in other words, simply relying on breathing exercises that can work for those who do not have enough variety and intensity of a Variety of stressors is not enough, even with breathing exercises, even if practiced frequently, it can be handled effectively.

Similarly, a stress management program that includes a wide range of proven techniques may not be effective if the techniques are so challenging and challenging that they are not learned properly and are not used regularly. You need a plan that suits you with a variety of stressors and the amount of time and energy you have to learn and practice the techniques.

Build Your Plan: Find the Right Combination

Naturally, we all find ways to deal with stress, but some strategies are more effective than others. (Contacting friends for help and having that friend available if you need to become a professional can be a healthier way to manage stress than baking chocolate cakes, although both activities can be instinctively attractive.) Find the key an optimal program is stress balance management.

All activities bring a mix of pros and cons, and finding the best balance of both is part of your adventure planning adventure strategy. (For example, exercise or meditation diets bring many benefits, but they require energy and time; visualization may take less time and energy, but entails a different level of reimbursement.) Part of creating a stress management plan is to find a balance between the benefits. You are looking for it and you enable your level of time and effort.

Planning for the future is also important. If you wait until you feel stressed, you can resort to fewer stress reactions (chocolate cake, anyone?) Instead of using proven and effective approaches that can help you manage your stress more effectively. However, if you have already created a program, one that addresses your personality, lifestyle and specific needs will facilitate stress management in any way you want. We will take the next step and assemble that map.

An Ideal Plan

The ideal stress management plan will be unique. Depending on what you already enjoy doing, the type of stress you need to drive and a number of other factors, you may find something completely different from what your best friend is doing or what he may be creating for 10 years. . . This is good; We have many techniques to choose from and the design can evolve like you.

Since we started creating an application, you can ask yourself the following questions to meet your needs and what techniques might work for you:

— How quickly do I need to get rid of stress? (This can help you decide between focusing more on quick-relief medications or spending time on techniques that can reduce your stress level gradually but permanently over time.)

— How much time do I invest in learning new techniques?

— How much stress do I have to handle?

— Do I experience this short-term stress, or do I generally experience this level of stress?

— What areas of my life cause stress?

— Do I prefer to do my best to eliminate stressors from my life, whenever possible, or concentrate on resisting stressors that occur to me?

After answering these questions, reading the previous chapters and reviewing your life, you should have some ideas on where to start. Here are some other thoughts to consider when planning the final plan to deal with your stress. While you are eventually developing a list of new habits to adopt, or reviewing a list that you have previously developed, you may want this program to meet the following criteria:

— A combination of short and long term techniques. Ideally, if you have some techniques that can meet the short-term needs of your response to short-term stress and the long-term need to increase stress resistance in general, you can effectively manage stress Unless you meet only one of these needs. (Note that it is true

— Both stress relieving drugs are used for both purposes. This is very useful and can help you start where you want to start your program.)

— A plan that suits your specific needs. If you are interested in a set of techniques that you can use in different situations, developing a multilayer approach may work very well. If you feel you have learned only two or three new techniques in the near future, be honest with yourself and plan it. Be realistic with what you want and can do and are likely to do the same. (That said, keep in mind that there are at least two strategies to reverse if one does not work for all situations).

— You need the areas where you need more help. Avoid dealing with stressful areas because exposure to stress is intimidating. You may not be ready at this time to break some toxic relationships or start a long-term exercise habit at this time, but if these are the strategies that will relieve some of your areas of greatest stress, I will encourage you to take notes of this. Try it in the future and maybe it's in tune.

— Create a flexible plan. Allow yourself extra time to advance each step if necessary. For example, if you need to gather more information before you feel ready to take action, do so. If you discover that it goes back to old habits, remind yourself that this can happen and that re-acceptance is part of the process. You don't ask for perfection yourself, but you hope to keep your goals. Remember that you are in the long term business.

Questions to Ask Yourself

These questions are often found at the end of the chapter, but in this case, as you are likely to decide on the changes you want to make, it will help you make some discoveries before moving on to the next step. Here are some questions to think about:

— What parts of your life will benefit most from the change at this time?

— What changes could be easier?

— What changes could be more beneficial?

— What changes are better if I start as soon as possible?

— Do I feel changed in the next few days, the next weeks or the next months?

— Do I need more information before deciding on an internship? If so, what questions will be answered?

— Have I tried to make this change in the past (if a goal was identified) or repeated or gave up? If so, what did I learn from the process?

— What resources can help me change?

Conclusion

Congratulations on making it to the end of this ***Stress Management: Be Calm and Stop Feeling Overwhelmed*** navigation guide. I hope you'll find the information as useful and helpful.

Stress management is not only a dire need in today's fast-paced lifestyle, but also a crucial factor in physical and mental health. It is one of the most weakening emotions we can have. Stress is a psychological approach that teaches people the skills they need to cope with anxiety and stress. Not only mental stress, but also many cases that can lead to physical health problems, both short and long term.

One sad thing about stress is often not as stressful as stress itself, although it is very unpleasant for the person to get stressed, but the fear of the reaction of others if they want to have confidence in a friend, family or co-worker, even professionals of stress management.

At equal time, we all realize the effects that pressure can have, and in case you examine this book in search of a treatment or at least an alleviation from personal pressure or a cherished one, the effects of strain need no similarly explanation.

As you have got learned, stress control begins by figuring out the assets of stress for your existence. It isn't as easy as it looks. The actual assets of your strain are not usually obvious and it's far very smooth to ignore your thoughts, emotions and strain behaviors.

Another sad fact about stress management, and being a stress and anger management specialist myself and I know it very well, is the widespread belief that stress management doesn't matter. That is a "spongy" concept that is not necessary, or only for the weak.

Stress management is critical for success at work and for a healthy life. Stress management is constantly increasing due to our kind of busy schedules today.

To your success!

Made in the USA
San Bernardino, CA
10 January 2020